THE ILLUSTRATED DINOSAUR ENCYCLOPEDIA

DOUGAL DIXON

ILLUSTRATED BY
ANDREW ROBINSON & DAVID JOHNSTON

WHSMITH
EXCLUSIVE
· BOOKS ·

This edition first published in Great Britain in 1988 by
Octopus Books Ltd
Michelin House
81 Fulham Road
London SW3 6RB

Relief maps by Brian Watson

Additional maps and diagrams by Janos Marffy

ISBN 0 7064 3238 X

This edition produced exclusively for W.H. Smith

Printed in Italy

CONTENTS

CONTENTS

HOW TO USE THIS BOOK

The animals in this book are arranged chronologically – that is, in the order in which they appeared in geological time. The earliest appeared in the Triassic, then the early Jurassic, late Jurassic, early Cretaceous, and the last of them lived in late Cretaceous times.

Each animal is given a double-page spread to itself, a spread on which we can see what the animal looked like in life, how it lived, and what we can tell from the skeleton. A fact box tells what part of the world it lived in, and a bit about the history of its discovery. Each title heading is colour-keyed as well, to give an indication of what kind of dinosaur it was.

As we can see from page 14-15 the dinosaurs are classified into two different orders – the Saurischia, or the lizard-hipped dinosaurs, and the Ornithischia, or the bird-hipped dinosaurs. These are further subdivided as follows, and the subdivisions are accompanied by their colour key.

Each fact box starts off with some technical information. For example:

STEGOCERAS VALIDUS
(Full species name)

'VALID HORNED ROOF'
(Literal translation of species name)

PACHYCEPHALOSAURIA (Suborder)
PACHYCEPHALOSAURID (Family)

LATE CRETACEOUS
(Time in which it lived)

WESTERN NORTH AMERICA
(Place where remains have been found)

ORDER SAURISCHIA

SUBORDER THEROPODA meat-eating dinosaurs

SUBORDER SAUROPODOMORPHA long-necked plant-eating dinosaurs

ORDER ORNITHISCHIA

SUBORDER ORNITHOPODA two-footed plant-eating dinosaurs

SUBORDER PACHYCEPHALOSAURIA bone-headed dinosaurs

SUBORDER ANKYLOSAURIA armoured plant-eating dinosaurs

SUBORDER STEGOSAURIA plated plant-eating dinosaurs

SUBORDER CERATOPSIA horned plant-eating dinosaurs

LOOKING BACK THROUGH TIME

Think of an animal.

Think of all the animals you have seen or heard about.

Think of the tropical forests with trees screeching with monkeys and parrots, and a damp dark undergrowth where forest hogs and anteaters scurry. Think of the sweeping grasslands with the seething herds of wildebeest and zebra, stalked by lions and cheetahs. Think of the deserts, with snakes slithering through the sand and jerboas bouncing, kangaroo-like, over the rocks. Think of the temperate woodlands, and the coniferous forests, where deer and moose browse and through which the wolves hunt in stealthy packs. Then think of the chill tundra and the icy wastes of the North Pole, where reindeer migrate to spend the long days of the cool, mosquito-laden summer and polar bears hunt seals through the ice.

You are looking at a picture of life frozen in a moment of geological time.

Now, turn the clock back five million years, to a time when our ancestors were indistinguishable from the apes, and look again. You will see another picture, every bit as complex and varied, but with totally different sets of animals living in the forests, the grasslands, the deserts, and each of the other environments. Monkeys and parrots would be there, but not the monkeys and parrots we would know. Different types of hunting cat would be stalking unfamiliar antelopes through the grasslands. Turn the clock back another five million years and the animal life will be totally different again, and even more unfamiliar. And again for five million years before that...

The animal life that we have today is just a snapshot of the whole vast parade of life on our planet. We have met only a tiny proportion of all the types of animals that have existed since life began three and a half thousand million years ago – a period of time representing 700 of our five-million-year jumps.

One of the groups of ancient animals that we find most fascinating is the dinosaur group. This came into existence about 220 or 230 million years ago, flourished for about 160 million years and disappeared suddenly a mere 65 million years ago.

The world itself has also changed. We have all been to a familiar place and found that something in the landscape has altered – the bend of a river silted up, or a piece of a cliff fallen into the sea. If changes like this can happen within a few years of human memory, think of the changes that can take place over the thousands of millions of years of the Earth's history.

To try to read the story of the Earth and of the animals and plants that have lived on it would seem to be a hopeless task – there are no records or documents or photographs surviving from these times. Yet the ancient landscapes and the ancient life-forms have left us their own testimony.

Some basic geology first of all. The Earth's crust is made up of several types of rock, but the only one that interests us here is called SEDIMENTARY rock. This forms as layers of sand, gravel, mud or other debris becomes buried, compressed and cemented together into a solid mass.

Different sediments form under different conditions. Fragments of limy rubble will gather around a coral reef. Layers of dark mud will accumulate on the ocean floor. Pebbles will be washed up on a shingle beach. These may eventually form sedimentary rocks – limestone, shale and conglomerate respectively. A geologist looking at these rocks will be able to imagine the coral reef, the ocean floor and the shingle beach from what he sees. Different kinds of sand can form on the seashore, on a river bed or in a desert. These sands may eventually become sandstones when the conditions change, and each sandstone will be different from the other and quite recognizable to the geologist.

Over the centuries geologists have mapped the sedimentary rocks and determined their ages relative to one another. From these observations they have compiled the geological time scale, which is an easy way to talk about the vast sweeps of geological time. The time scale is divided into large spans called eras and smaller spans called periods. There are also finer divisions still, but for our purposes the periods will suffice. The Mesozoic Era was the age of dinosaurs, and each Mesozoic period – the Triassic, Jurassic and Cretaceous – had its own distinctive dinosaur fauna.

▶ **The geological time scale is a convenient chart used to plot the course of the history of our planet. All the dinosaurs lived in the Mesozoic era – The Triassic, Jurassic and Cretaceous periods.**

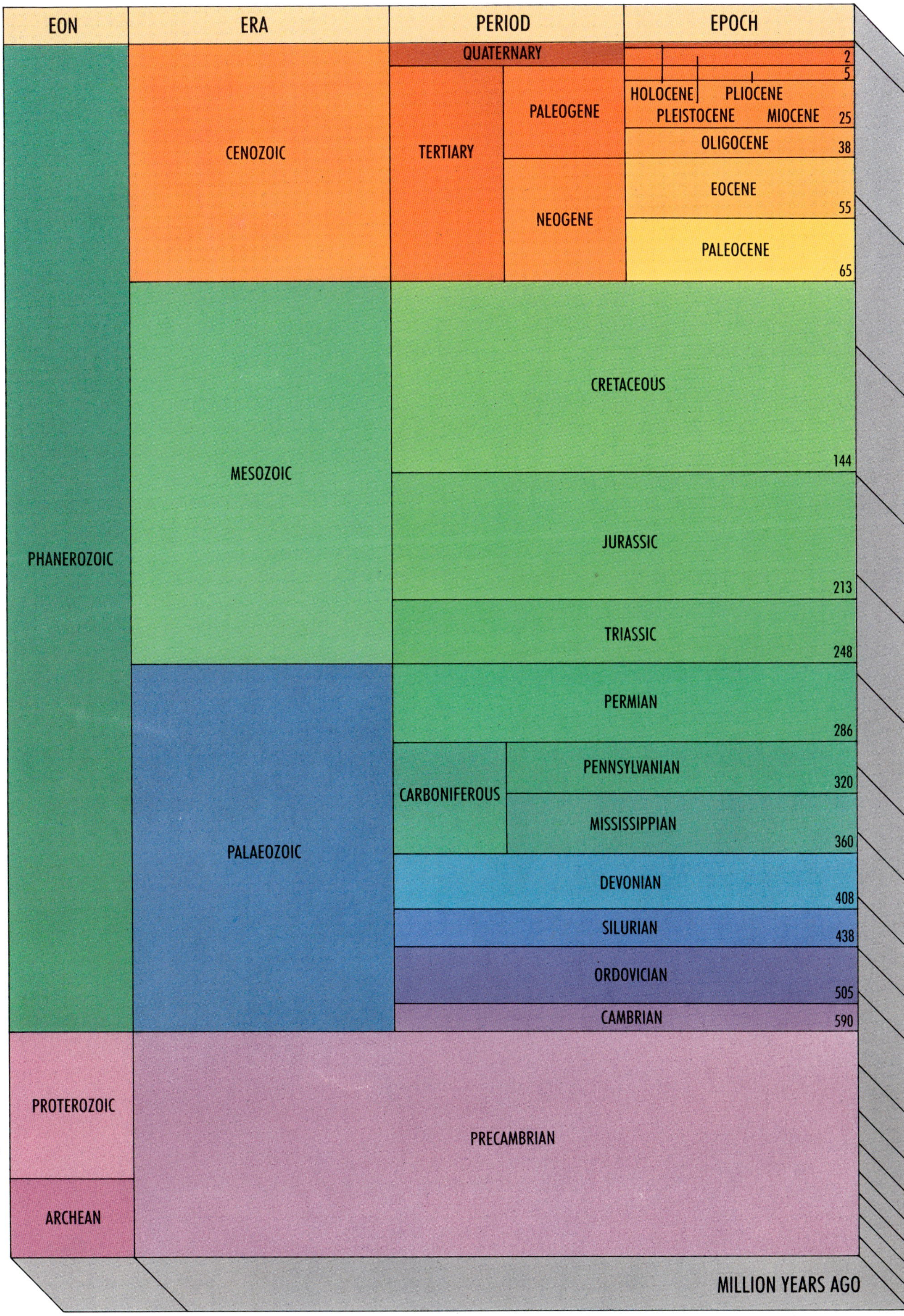
EON
ERA
PERIOD
EPOCH
QUATERNARY
2
5
HOLOCENE
PLIOCENE
PALEOGENE
PLEISTOCENE
MIOCENE
25
CENOZOIC
TERTIARY
OLIGOCENE
38
EOCENE
55
NEOGENE
PALEOCENE
65
CRETACEOUS
144
MESOZOIC
JURASSIC
213
PHANEROZOIC
TRIASSIC
248
PERMIAN
286
PENNSYLVANIAN
320
CARBONIFEROUS
MISSISSIPPIAN
360
PALAEOZOIC
DEVONIAN
408
SILURIAN
438
ORDOVICIAN
505
CAMBRIAN
590
PROTEROZOIC
PRECAMBRIAN
ARCHEAN
MILLION YEARS AGO
0.01
50
100
150
200
250
300
350
400
450
500
1,000
1,500
2,000
2,500
3,000
3,500
4,000

FOSSILS

When an animal dies it rots. Vultures and crows rip away the decaying flesh and innards, flies and bacteria polish up what is left, and the bones eventually decay in the sun and the rain. Nothing is left.

Occasionally, however, the body will end up in a place where it may be preserved. It may fall into a flooded river and be immediately buried by sand. The vultures and crows may then miss it, and the flies and bacteria may not have a chance to do their work. These circumstances are rare – perhaps one body in several hundred thousand may end up like this. But it does happen, and when it does the body is ready to become a fossil.

Fossilization can happen in several different ways. Under very special circumstances the animal may become preserved whole and unaltered. We see this in mammoths that have become entombed in frozen mud during the Ice Age, and in insects caught in resin oozing from coniferous trees and preserved when the resin turned to amber in the ground. Dinosaurs cannot be fossilized in this way, because they all died out before the Ice Age – and they couldn't climb trees!

Under other rare circumstances only part of the creature may be preserved, but that part may be preserved without any alteration. Bones of Ice Age mammals have been found in natural tar pits in Los Angeles, USA, and sharks' teeth are often found in Tertiary sea deposits. These remains are relatively young in geological terms and, again, this does not happen to dinosaur remains.

Even when an animal or plant is rapidly buried and preserved, the geological changes in the rock will eventually break down the once living substance. Sometimes, however, some of the original material is left. Fern leaves and twigs are sometimes preserved as a thin black film of the original carbon when all the other chemicals have seeped away. Plants may be preserved like this – not dinosaurs.

Sometimes, when a bone is buried and entombed in sedimentary rock, water seeping through the rock may deposit minerals in the bone. The bone itself may break down, molecule by molecule, but at the same time it is replaced by the new mineral, molecule by molecule. The result is a fossil bone that still has all its microscopic structure, but made of a totally new mineral substance, such as silica. Now we are coming to the type of fossilization

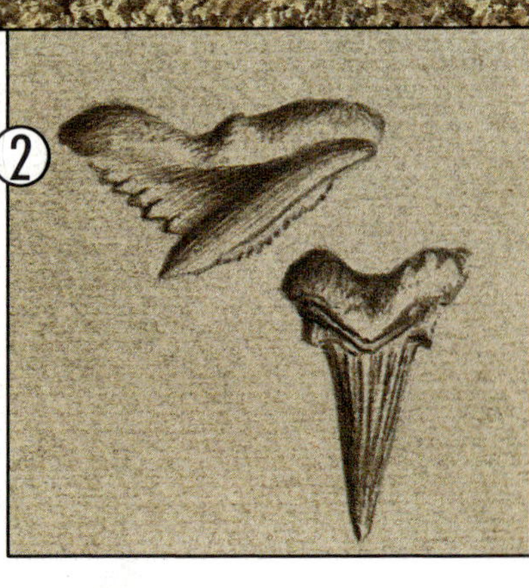

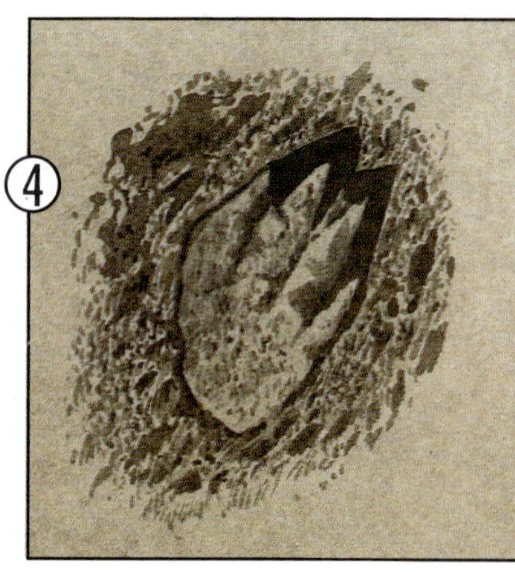

▲ Animals or plants may be preserved as fossils in a number of different ways. Once in a while the whole organism is preserved in its entirety like the mammoths in the frozen mud of Siberia (1), or only the hard parts may remain, such as the bones of the animals trapped in tar pits (2). Sometimes, some of the original substance is left while the rest decays away, such as the carbon from substance of leaves (3).

that can preserve dinosaurs.

Then again, the bone in the sedimentary rock may decompose completely leaving a hole, called a mould, within the rock. Later, the groundwater seeping through the rock may fill up the mould with a mineral, such as calcite, and form a mineral lump in the exact shape of the original bone. This shape is called a cast, and does not show the original microscopic structure of the bone. Again, dinosaur bones may be found as moulds or casts.

A fossil need not be part of the animal at all. Trace fossils are formed when an animal digs a tunnel in sand or crawls across a beach. When the sand is turned to sandstone the tracks and tunnels are preserved as shapes in the rock. Dinosaur footprints are examples of these trace fossils.

Although dinosaur bones can be found as fossils, it is very unlikely that the entire skeleton will be preserved, still joined together. Usually the body decays away quite quickly or is pulled to bits by scavenging animals. The bones, being harder and more durable, may have a chance to be swept up in a flood at a later time and buried. Entire fossil skeletons are found occasionally as a result of the animal being buried immediately after death.

This illustrates the different kinds of fossil constructions, or assemblages, recognized by the geologist. A DEATH ASSEMBLAGE will be a collection of disarticulated bones, mixed up with bits of shells and other animals that have been washed in from other areas. A LIFE ASSEMBLAGE, on the other hand, has the skeletons still whole, along with other animals from that area and plants that are still in the position in which they grew. The latter is by far the more useful kind of assemblage, since it tells the geologist much more about the lifestyles of the creatures concerned.

▲ A mounted dinosaur skeleton in a museum gives us a good idea of what ancient animals were like.

Sometimes, although rarely, a fossil can show dramatic indications of the lifestyle of an animal. A fossil bone may be ripped and scratched by the teeth of a huge meat-eating animal, and the broken teeth may be found nearby. This shows that the animal had been set upon by some fearsome meat-eater. Sometimes a well-preserved skeleton will still have the remains of its last meal in its stomach area, giving us an insight into its diet. Sometimes two different animals will be preserved locked together, teeth and claws bared – the result of a struggle to the death that killed them both.

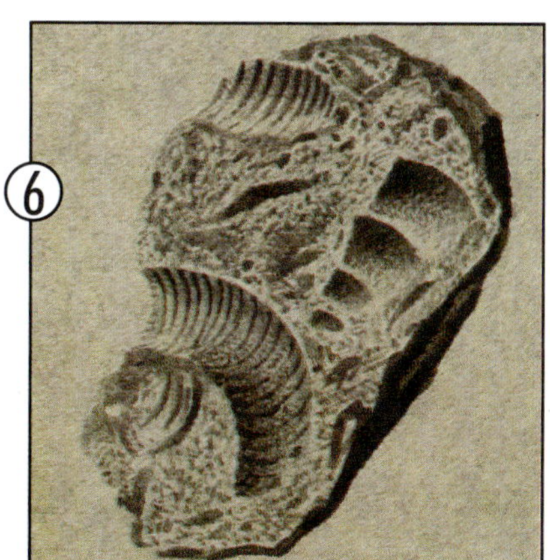

In petrifaction the once-living substance, such as bone, is replaced by mineral (4). When a fossil decays away it leaves a hole in the rock called a mould (5), and when this is filled with minerals it forms a solid shape called a cast (6) which is the same shape as the original. A trace fossil (7) represents a mark made by an ancient animal as it moved over the sediment.

LIFE EVOLVES

For a long time geologists and palaeontologists have been studying the fossils in the different layers of rock and building up a picture of the progress of life throughout the history of our planet. The picture is far from complete. Every year, every expedition, every research project produces new information.

The first living things were present about 3500 million years ago, when our planet was still young. We do not know how they came into being, but we know they were there. The first life would probably have been nothing more than a complex chemical molecule that had the power to make a copy of itself from the chemicals round about. It would have been able to break down other chemicals and put the atoms together in a mirror image of itself, and this mirror image would, in turn, have had the same reproductive power. Only if the copy were perfect would it be able to reproduce itself. An imperfect copy would not have reproduced and would have become extinct. On the other hand, if any random change in the reproduced molecule helped in the reproducing process, then this change would be carried on to the next stage. That change would be present when the next molecule reproduced, and so on. Evolution had begun.

As time went on, the molecules became more and more efficient and more and more complex. They could remain still and use the energy of the sun to make their own raw materials from the chemicals round about. Hence, the first plants. Otherwise they could move to find the raw materials already made. Hence, the first animals. All this went on in Precambrian times and we do not really know much about it. All the early animals and plants were soft bodied

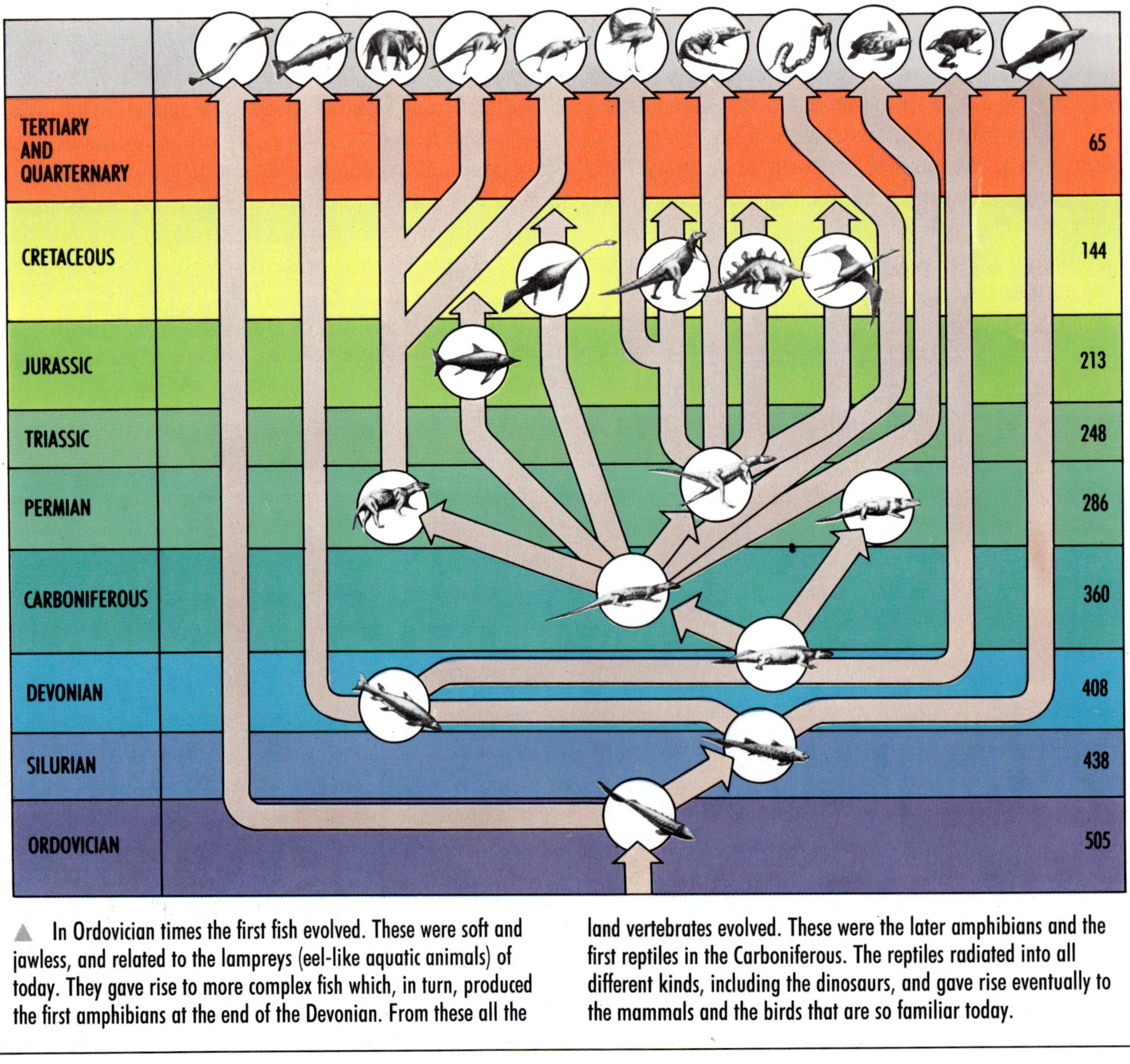

▲ In Ordovician times the first fish evolved. These were soft and jawless, and related to the lampreys (eel-like aquatic animals) of today. They gave rise to more complex fish which, in turn, produced the first amphibians at the end of the Devonian. From these all the land vertebrates evolved. These were the later amphibians and the first reptiles in the Carboniferous. The reptiles radiated into all different kinds, including the dinosaurs, and gave rise eventually to the mammals and the birds that are so familiar today.

and did not fossilize at all well. It is not until the beginning of the Cambrian period, 590 million years ago, that we find good fossils. At this time animals with hard shells suddenly evolved. Everything at that time lived in the sea, and their fossils are found in sea sediments. There were, however, no animals with backbones.

Shortly afterwards a worm-like creature evolved, which had a stiffening bar of gristle along its length. From this bar a backbone evolved, the worm segments became stiffened into ribs, and a skull protected the brain at the head end. This was the first fish.

Changes to the ribs produced jaws, gill supports and limb girdles with fins, and the fish began to look like fish that we would recognize.

The next step was a big one. In the early days, the Earth's atmosphere consisted largely of carbon dioxide. While the primitive plants were busily using the sunlight to power their food factories, they produced oxygen as a by-product. This oxygen built up in the atmosphere until it was concentrated enough to support animal life (for animal life needs oxygen as much as plant life needs sunlight). Land animals then evolved.

The first fish to do this had lungs that could work in air, and the fins were muscular and arranged in pairs so that the fish could pull itself over the ground. By this time it was the Devonian period, and there was a flourishing growth of plant life, and hence food, on land.

From this lung fish it was a short step to the first amphibian. This had legs instead of fins and could spend its adult life on land, breathing air. However, it had bred in the water, and its young stage was a water-dwelling tadpole.

The first reptile evolved in the Carboniferous period. It would have looked very much like the amphibians of the time, but it laid a hard-shelled egg on land. This egg acted like a miniature pool for the tadpole, and so the reptile did not need to live in water for any part of its life.

The reptile group expanded dramatically from then onward. Some became warm-blooded and hairy and bore their young alive. These eventually developed into the mammals. Some abandoned the land life and went back to living in the sea. These became the ichthyosaurs and the plesiosaurs. Some grew hard shells and became the modern tortoises and turtles. Some remained small and unspecialized, while some lost their legs and took up a burrowing or slithering existence. They became today's lizards and snakes. Some remained unchanged since their early days and lived as armoured semi-aquatic meat-eaters – the crocodiles. Some took up the power of flight and became the pterosaurs. Finally, two very specialized groups spread to populate the land, and produced some of the most spectacular and successful animals that ever walked the Earth. These were the dinosaurs.

▼ A virus is the simplest and the smallest of living things. It consists merely of a protective case containing a complex molecule that can reproduce.

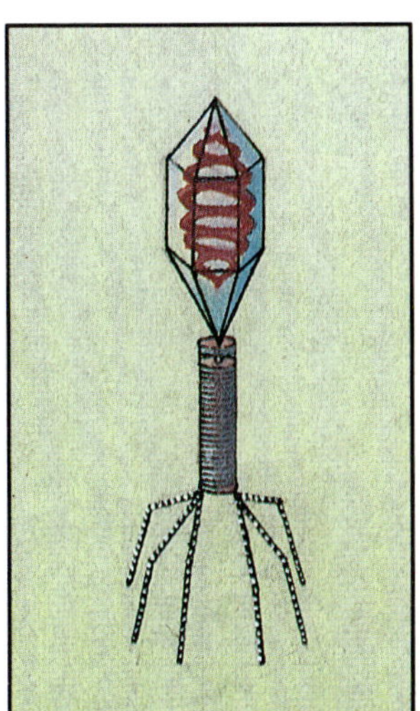

▼ A living cell has a nucleus of reproductive molecules, surrounded by a bag of jelly-like protoplasm. The amoeba is an animal with just a single cell.

▼ Most creatures have many cells. In the alga *Volvox*, a number of cells are loosely bound together, but each one is exactly the same.

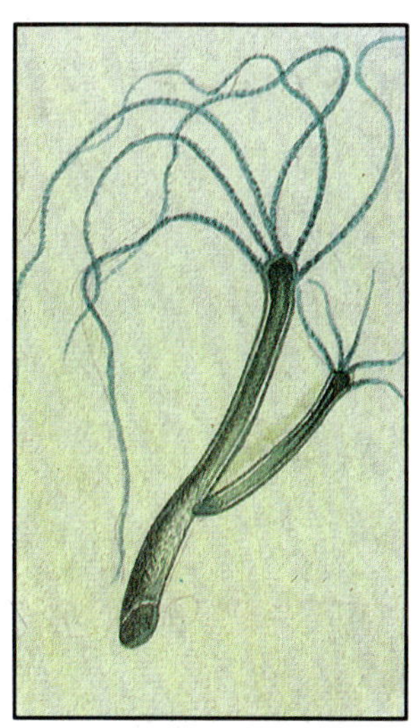

▼ Complex creatures have different structures called organs, e.g. eyes and wings, made from matter we call tissue, which is made up of different kinds of cells.

THE DINOSAUR

What is a dinosaur?

The word 'dinosaur' is a difficult one to define. It does not have any scientific meaning. It covers two different orders of animals – the Saurischia and the Ornithischia – which are about as closely related to each other as they are to the extinct pterosaurs and to the still living crocodiles. These four orders – the Saurischia, Ornithischia, Pterosauria and Crocodilia – are regarded as a major group called the Archosauria, or the ruling reptiles.

The archosaurs evolved from a group of Triassic reptiles called the thecodonts. These were rather lizard-like or crocodile-like but differed from the other reptiles by having each tooth in the jaw growing from its individual socket, rather than having them growing from the surface of the jawbone. This may seem a minor point, but it does make the thecodonts different from the other reptile groups. The thecodonts were themselves quite a varied group, consisting of squat, sprawling animals, crocodile-like swimming meat-eaters and even some gliding forms. Perhaps the most typical was a 60 cm (2 ft) lizard-like creature called *Euparkeria*. This was basically a four-footed animal, but when moving fast it would have been able to lift itself up on its hind legs and sprint across the desert sands. In appearance it must have resembled a tiny version of the great two-footed dinosaurs to come.

From the thecodonts there developed the conservative crocodile group and the flying pterosaurs. There also developed the saurischians and the ornithischians.

Although *Euparkeria* may have resembled a little dinosaur itself, it differed in one important feature. Its legs still stuck out at the side like those of other reptiles. The saurischian and ornithischian legs were held directly beneath the body, more like those of mammals. This meant that the legs of saurischians and ornithischians could support the weight of a very large body. A lizard could not have grown very large, since a lizard's legs stick out at the side and the body is slung between them. This gives a lizard a peculiar sprawling stance, and the leverage of the legs is wrong for supporting big bodies. A dinosaur, on the other hand, could be very heavy, since its body was above and on top of the legs, and the weight could bear down vertically through them. Imagine the heavy body of an elephant, supported on its pillar-like legs. That works well. Now try to imagine the same weight slung between legs that stick out at the side. The animal would collapse! It was this physical arrangement of the legs that enabled some dinosaurs to grow huge.

The saurischians and ornithischians differed from one another in the shape of the hip bones. The saurischians (the name means 'lizard-hipped') had a pelvic girdle that consisted of a pair of flat bones at the top, attached to the backbone – ilium bones. Then, from the sockets into which the leg bones fitted, a pair of bones pointed down and backwards – ischium bones – and a pair of pubis bones pointed down and forward. The first saurischians were meat-eaters. They walked on two legs, leaving their forelimbs to grasp their prey. When they rested, their bodies lay on the ground supported by the strong pubis bone.

From these creatures evolved plant-eating saurischians. Since plant eating needs a much larger gut than meat eating, the body had to be so much larger. There was then a heavy body

▶ Primitive reptiles have legs that stick out sideways (left). Crocodiles can lift their bodies clear of the ground in a semi-erect stance (centre). Dinosaurs and mammals were able to walk straight-legged (right). The early archosaurs were aquatic-like crocodiles. They developed strong hind legs and long tails to help them swim. On land, their descendants were able to walk on their strong hind legs, balanced by their long tails.

before the hips and the animal could not balance on two legs any more. It took up a four-footed existence. The meat-eating saurischians are called the THEROPODS (or 'mammal footed') while the heavy long-necked plant-eating saurischians are called the SAUROPODS (or 'lizard footed').

The ornithischian (or 'bird-hipped') dinosaurs had the hip bones arranged differently. The pair of ilium bones and ischium bones were in the same position, but the pubis bones were swept back parallel to the ischium pair. This left a great gap beneath the hip structure. Since all the ornithischians were plant-eaters, the huge gut could fit into this gap and lie between the hind legs. Thus, the ornithischian could eat plants and still balance on its hind legs. The ORNITHOPOD ('bird-footed') ornithischians were built like this. Later, some took up a four-footed existence and became armoured in one way or another. The STEGOSAURS ('roofed lizards') had spikes and plates down the centre of the back, the ANKYLOSAURS ('welded lizards') had a broad mosaic of back armour, and the CERATOPSIANS ('horned heads') had armour and horns confined to the face and skull. The other main difference between the saurischians and ornithischians was in the skull. The ornithischian skull had an extra bone on the lower jaw – the predentary – which held a horny beak.

The bird-like hip of the ornithischians probably evolved from the lizard-like hip of the saurischians. However, the bird-like hip arrangement seems to have evolved several times independently. A group of meat-eating dinosaurs recently discovered had a hip arrangement that was distinctly ornithischian, although they were quite definitely saurischian dinosaurs. During the Jurassic period another group of animals with bird-like hips evolved from the saurischians. These were the birds themselves.

▼ The lizard-like hip of the plant-eating saurischian dinosaur.

▲ The bird-like hip of the plant-eating ornithischian dinosaur.

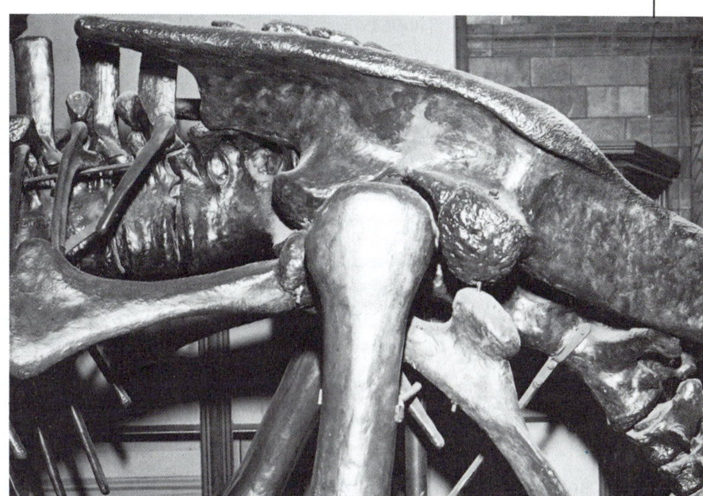

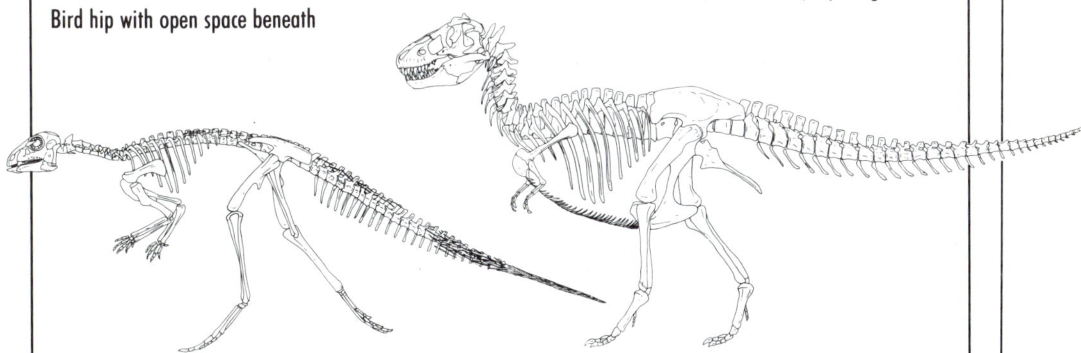

▶ The lizard-like hip of the saurischian dinosaur was a mass of bone that radiated away from the point of attachment of the leg. For a plant-eating saurischian the heavy body with the complex digestive system had to be held well forward of it. The bird-like hip of the plant-eating ornithischian dinosaur had a gap beneath it. This meant that the heavy body could be quite compact and could balance at the hips.

EARTH – THE MOVING SURFACE

The animal and plant life of the Earth's surface changed considerably through geological time. But the Earth's surface itself changed just as dramatically. We must now say a few words about this changing backdrop to the story of life on our planet.

The Earth's crust is on the move. For two hundred years people have suspected as much. If you look at a map of the world, some of the continents – particularly South America and Africa – seem to fit into one another like pieces of a jigsaw. From this we can presume that all the continents were once one single land mass and that at some time in the past this supercontinent split up and the pieces moved apart. This concept was known as CONTINENTAL DRIFT.

Then in the 1960s, it was discovered that the ocean floors were expanding. Through each ocean lies an ocean ridge, with submarine volcanoes along its length. Geologists discovered that the rocks of the ridge were new, and that away from the ridge crest they became older and older. Likewise, the sediments that had settled on the sea floor were thin over the ridge and became thicker further away. These observations, as well as other lines of evidence, indicated that the ocean basins were growing from their ridges. New crust was being produced by the volcanic activity at the ridge crests and moving away at each side as yet newer crust was formed in between. This concept was known as SEAFLOOR SPREADING.

The ideas of continental drift and seafloor spreading were then combined in the all-embracing concept of PLATE TECTONICS. Imagine the surface of the Earth as consisting of a number of plates, like the panels of a football. Each plate is being continually generated along one seam and moving away from its neighbour.

▶ We can picture the surface of the Earth as being made up of a number of different plates. These are all growing from the ocean ridges and are being swallowed up along ocean trenches. The continents are carried here and there by this movement.

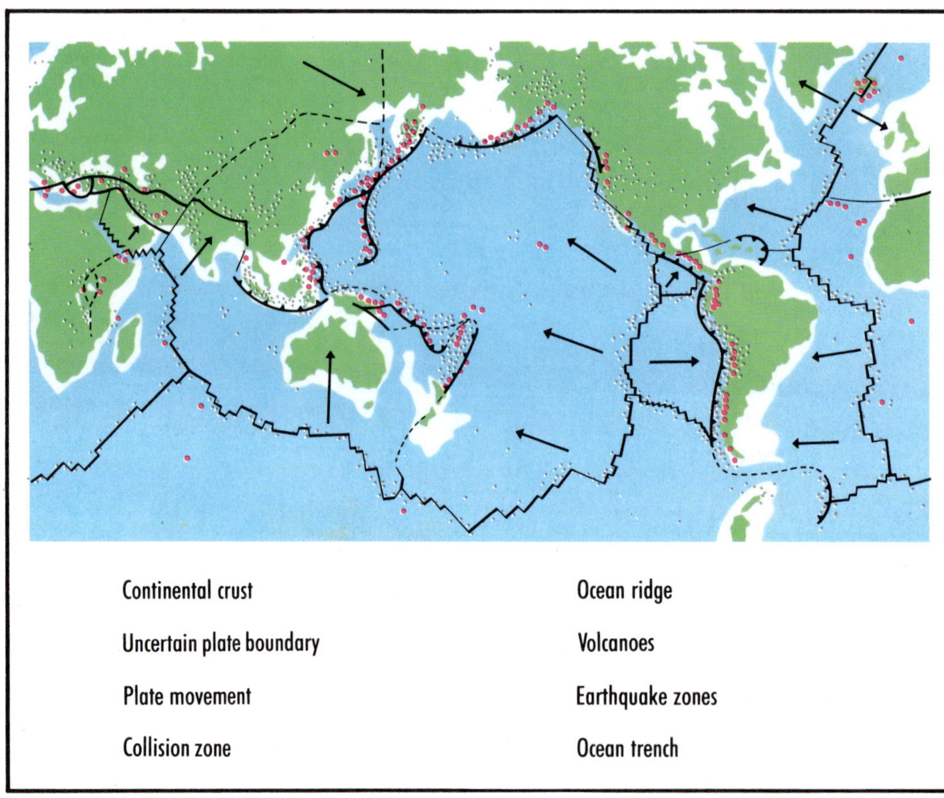

▼ An idealized cross section of a plate. New plate material, moving to the left from the ocean ridge, is being swallowed up beneath an old plate along an ocean trench, and an arc of volcanic islands is being formed there. The plate moving right is being swallowed up beneath a continent and mountains are forming. At the far right, two continents collide to produce a mountain range.

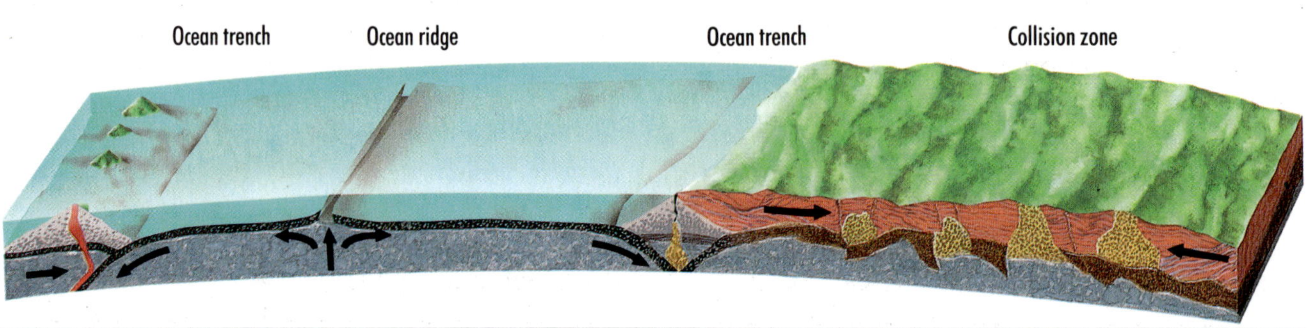

◄ The lower beds in this cliff in Wyoming, USA, were formed in Triassic times. They were then lifted up and worn down to a flat landscape surface. Then, in the Tertiary, the landscape became a sea bed and the top beds were laid down on it. The line dividing the two groups of beds is called an unconformity.

▼ Sedimentary rocks are laid down in layers, called strata, with the oldest at the bottom and the youngest at the top. Each stratum may tell a different story about changing conditions.

▲ Mud cracks, formed where an ancient pond dried out in the sun, may be preserved in sedimentary rock strata.

▼ When old desert sands are eventually turned into sandstones, we can often see the shapes of the sand-dunes preserved in them.

Where two moving plates meet at the opposite seam one plunges down beneath the other and is destroyed in the Earth's interior. This is what is happening to the plates of the oceanic crust. Where the plates are being generated – the constructive plate margins – there are oceanic ridges. Where they are being swallowed up – the destructive margins – there are oceanic trenches. Earthquakes and volcanoes are found at all these margins.

And the continents? They are made of a much lighter material than the oceanic crust. They are embedded in the moving ocean material and are carried here and there like logs embedded in the ice of a frozen river. When they are carried to a destructive margin they stop, since they are too light to be pulled down into the Earth's interior. Thus we often find ocean trenches just offshore, such as down the west coast of South America. Volcanic mountain ranges – in this case the Andes – form there because of the crushing effect of the movement. When two continents collide they become welded together, and a vast mountain range is crushed up between them. The Himalayas formed where India collided with Asia during the Tertiary period.

Geologists can plot the movements of the continents at various points in geological time. Magnetic minerals in the rocks can tell where the continents were in relation to the magnetic poles when the rocks were formed.

So, plate tectonics can show us where the continental blocks were at a particular geological period. However, this does not give us much idea about the actual geographies of those continents. The edge of the continent is not the edge of the land. Usually, the sea covers the continental edge for a distance of up to several hundred kilometres, forming the continental shelf. The positions of the actual ancient coastlines are difficult to work out. We must look at the sedimentary rocks formed at particular areas at particular times. Then we can come up with a generalized picture of the distributions of shallow seas, river plains, deserts, mountains, ice caps, and all the other landscape features that go into making the geography of a particular continent. Some of the sedimentary rocks may even show us what the climate was like – desert sand dunes are often preserved, as are pits made by raindrops, mud cracks formed by droughts, and so on.

PRECAMBRIAN – A TIME OF MYSTERY

The further back in time we go, the less precise is our idea of what the Earth was like. The vast span of time we regard as the Precambrian – i.e. all the history of the Earth before the Cambrian period began 590 million years ago – is the haziest of all.

We can assume that the continents were scattered over the Earth's surface, moving, colliding into bigger continents, and then splitting up again, but we cannot see back far enough to plot them accurately. The central masses of each continent are made of Precambrian rocks, so we know that the continents were present back in those times. Most of the sedimentary rocks formed during this long time have long since been caught up in mountain-building activity and turned into metamorphic rocks. However, some sedimentary rocks, especially from the younger end of the Precambrian, have remained unchanged.

In the latter part of the Precambrian there was much mountain-building. Where we get mountains, we also get rivers flowing off them, and sand and gravel and mud being washed down to the sea. As a result there were large extents of sediments formed in the seas of the times and hence large masses of sedimentary rocks. These tend to be rich in iron ore – iron ore of a kind that could only form if there were very little oxygen in the atmosphere. There is also evidence of ice ages that affected the world in Precambrian times. The main ones seem to have occurred 2300 million, 900 million, 800 million and, finally, 600 million years ago, the last being right at the end of the Precambrian.

Precambrian life forms are known from fossils found in various parts of the world. In South Africa, in a sequence of rocks called the Fig Tree Cherts, there are the microscopic remains of things that look like bacteria, or tiny algae. These date from about 3200 million years ago and show that, by that time, life had advanced beyond the stage of the self-reproducing molecules.

▼ Most of lowland Canada consists of Precambrian rocks. These formed as sediments, which were then turned into sedimentary rocks. The rocks were later thrust up into mountains, and later still were worn flat. This accounts for their contorted appearance.

▲ Stromatolites, fossil (above) and modern (right), formed when mats of algae trapped layers of mud. These layers of mud and algae mats built up to form domes and hummocks.

The Gunflint Chert of 1900 million years ago in Canada shows the remains of many different forms of blue-green algae. These are very simple life-forms not much more complex than the bacteria and certainy not as advanced as the red and the green algae that we know as seaweed. There are also structures here called stromatolites. These form when a mat of blue-green algae lies on the surface of the sand or mud. The incoming tide washes more sand over the mat and it sticks to it in a layer. Then the algae grow over this new layer and another layer of sand is stuck to it at the next big tide. Eventually, small humps of sand and algae form, which have an onion-like structure built up layer by layer. This can be seen to happen today on the coast of Australia. Fossil stromatolites are very distinctive and show just one of the life-forms that had developed by 1900 million years ago.

More algae are known from Bitter Springs in the Northern Territory, Australia. These are about 1000 million years old. Many different types are known from here, including things that may be quite advanced green algae.

The Ediacara fossil assemblage from South Australia is 600 million years old – almost Cambrian in fact – and is the most spectacular collection of Precambrian organisms. They are all soft-bodied creatures and it is only through good fortune that the shapes of their bodies have actually become preserved. And what strange shapes they are! It is as if evolution were trying out all sorts of new types of animals, most of which did not quite work because no sign of them is found in later deposits. There were creatures that looked like worms, with big heads and segmented bodies. Some were disc-shaped, like jellyfish. Others were feather-like, like modern sea-pens, and grew from the sea floor. Another had a three-lobed shape that is found amongst no modern creatures. None of these things had hard skeletons, and so it is possible that they lived world-wide and have not been generally preserved. The important thing about the Ediacara fossils is that they show that, by this time, living things had become more than just single cells. Cells had become grouped together to form organs with particular functions, and the organs all combined to produce organisms. Similar kinds of creatures are found from rocks of the same age in the Midlands of England, South Wales, South Africa and Siberia.

▲ The Ediacara fossils consist of many strange shapes of animals. Flat, worm-like animals crawled over the deep sea sediments of the time, while feathery creatures grew upwards from the sea bed and animals like jellyfish swam above them.

LOWER PALAEOZOIC – LIFE FLOURISHES

The Lower, or early, Palaeozoic consists of the Cambrian, Ordovician and Silurian periods – from 590 to 408 million years ago.

The continents of South America, Africa, India, Antarctica and Australia were all fused together in one great supercontinent near the South Pole. Geologists give the name Gondwana to this supercontinent. The continent of Asia was in two parts, on the equator at different sides of the world from one another. North America, the region of Scandinavia, and Southern Europe were all island continents. The oceans between have been given names by the geologists, too. Between Gondwana and the island of southern Europe lay the Proto-Tethys, and between North America, Scandinavia and Southern Europe lay the Iapetus. The Iapetus ocean could be thought of as the forerunner of the Atlantic.

Throughout the lower Palaeozoic, the continents were moving around. The most significant movement was the coming together of North America and the parts of Europe, gradually closing up the Iapetus ocean.

While all this was going on, the edges of all of these continents become flooded. Shallow seas spread over the continental shelves, covering vast areas with marine sediments which we can now see as great thicknesses of sedimentary rocks. As continents move towards each other they tend to crumple and buckle up at their leading edges. Marine sediments are swept up in front of them and form mountain ranges as they advance. The northern parts of the Appalachians in North America were formed at this time as the Iapetus ocean began to close. Between the approaching continents there was a destructive plate margin, with oceanic crust being drawn down beneath the Earth's surface and destroyed. This gave rise to chains of volcanic islands in the region. The igneous rocks produced by these volcanoes in Ordovician times can be seen today in the mountains of Wales and in the Lake District of Northern

▼ Throughout the lower Palaeozoic the continents were slowly moving together and towards a vast supecontinent in the southern hemisphere. Shallow seas spread over the edges of the land masses.

▲ Trilobites and other creatures with hard skeletons lived on the Cambrian sea bed. There were also soft-bodied animals such as jellyfish and sponges.

▶ Plant life crept ashore during Silurian times. The first land plants evolved from seaweeds left at high tide that could survive until the next tide.

England. During the Ordovician there was an ice age. The sedimentary rocks formed from the rocky debris deposited by the glaciers can now be seen in South America.

The life of the Lower Palaeozoic was spectacular even though it was nearly all confined to the sea. At the beginning of the Cambrian all sorts of animals suddenly developed hard shells, and so they were easily fossilized. There were trilobites – segmented animals looking rather like woodlice with shells made of chitin. Chitin is a substance like our fingernails, and makes up the shells of today's insects, crabs, lobsters and the other invertebrates with jointed legs. Another creature with a chitin shell was the graptolite. This was a communal organism, with many individuals growing from one stalk. The shell was leaf-like or feather-like with each individual animal sitting in its own little cup. They floated in the Ordovician and Silurian oceans and sank to the floor when they died. Deep sea deposits of these times are full of graptolite fossils.

Other shells were made of calcite, the kind of substance that goes into today's bivalve seashells, such as cockles, mussels and scallops. These included bivalves like those of today, and brachiopods, which looked like the bivalves but were in no way related to them. The bivalves and brachiopods looked like one another because they had the same lifestyle – lying on the sea bed protected from their enemies by their shells and feeding by filtering food from sea water. Where two unrelated animals look like one another like this, the result is known as 'convergent evolution'. Other animals with calcite hard parts included octopus-like creatures in coiled and straight shells, sea-snails, crinoids and sea urchins – relatives of the starfish. There were also corals, but these were not like the reef-building corals of today. They were more like sea anemones in hard shells.

All these animals lived in the sea, particularly on the broad continental shelves, along with a large number of seaweeds. It was once thought that nothing lived on land in the lower Palaeozoic before the most primitive land plants came ashore during the Silurian period. However, there have been some tantalizing finds in the desert sands of the North American Ordovician continent. These include a kind of a burrow made by something that must have looked like a millipede. If millipedes lived on land during the Ordovician, then there must also have been some kind of land plant present on which they fed.

▼ Silurian fossils show that a great variety of animal and plant life lived in the shallow seas at the time. Trilobites still existed but there were also many cephalopods (octopus-like animals in shells) and gastropods (sea snails). There were also corals. Some of these were solitary and grew like sea anemones in shelly cups. Others grew communally, with many individuals growing together.

UPPER PALAEOZOIC – LAND IS COLONIZED

The Upper, or later, Palaeozoic consisted of the Devonian, Carboniferous and Permian periods. In the United States the Carboniferous is regarded as two periods – the earlier Mississippian and the later Pennsylvanian.

The movements of the continents were quite spectacular at this time. The Iapetus ocean finally disappeared as North America collided with Scandinavia. This threw up a massive mountain range along the join, like today's Himalayas. We can still see the remains of this mountain range in the northern Appalachians, the Highlands of Scotland, and the Norwegian mountains. Geologists call this mountain range the Caledonides, or the Caledonian Mountains. As this great mountain chain built up, the rain and the winds started breaking it down. Huge quantities of sand were carried down to the surrounding lowlands by streams and spread across the plains by rivers. Thick beds of desert and river sandstones date from this period. Land plants are known from Silurian times but in the Devonian they really took hold, especially along the river banks and by the shallow seas and lakes.

▲ Devonian, Carboniferous and Permian geography showed the coming together of the continents. The environmental conditions during these times ranged from lush swamps to arid deserts.

During Carboniferous times the spreading fans of sediment crept out over the shallow seas. Deltas and swamps covered great areas of the northern continents. Plant life was now abundant, and these swamps carried thick, steamy jungles of primitive plants. Creeks and backwaters were choked by reed-beds of giant horsetails. Huge trees that would have been unrecognizable to us, but were distantly related to the little fern-like plants we call club mosses, grew from the mudbanks and sandbars, their straight trunks reaching up through the green gloom to the spreading branches away overhead. Any land that was above water was covered by an undergrowth of ferns and tree-ferns. On highlands round about there grew groves of primitive conifer-like trees. This vast volume of growing green matter was eventually buried and turned into coal, becoming the coalfields of North America and Europe.

Towards the end of the Carboniferous the southern supercontinent of Gondwana moved northwards and collided with North America and Europe. The impact of the African section with North America produced the main portion of the Appalachians. Where Africa hit Europe there was a mountain chain called the Variscan Mountains, little of which remains today.

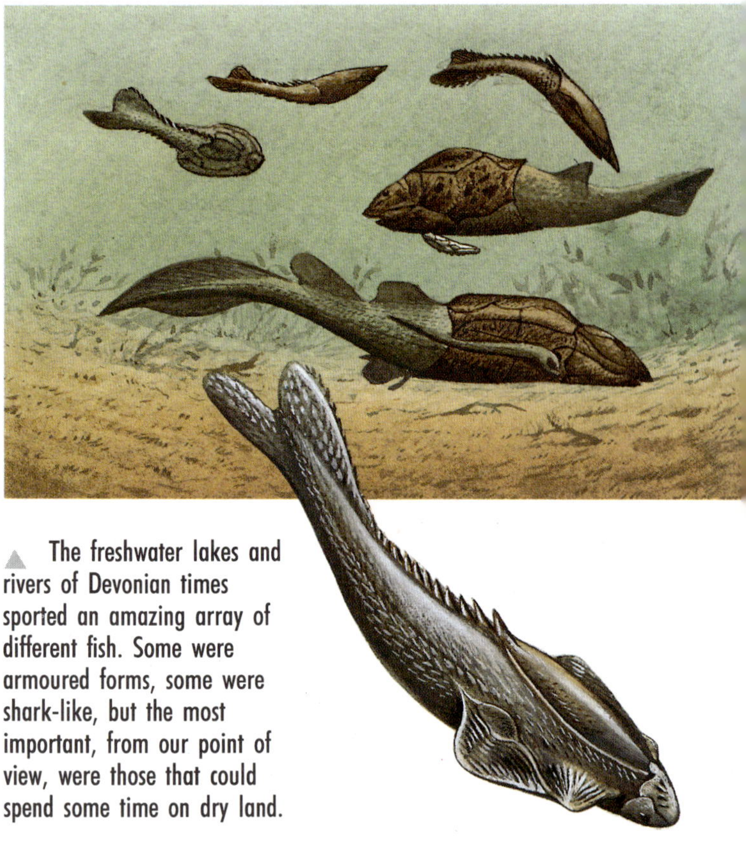

▲ The freshwater lakes and rivers of Devonian times sported an amazing array of different fish. Some were armoured forms, some were shark-like, but the most important, from our point of view, were those that could spend some time on dry land.

The next period, the Permian, was another time of deserts. It also saw the beginning of the time when all the continents of the Earth were fused together into one. This was achieved as Europe collided with northern Asia, throwing up the Ural Mountains where they fused together. Eastern Asia was now the only continental mass that was not part of the single great supercontinent. The shallow seas drained off the edges of the combined continents and huge areas of deserts developed. Another ice age also came and went in the south, leaving its deposits in South America, southern Africa, India, Antarctica and Australia.

Animal life continued to develop in the sea in the upper Palaeozoic, but it was on land that the big changes occurred. Many types of fish lived in the river estuaries and freshwater lakes of the Devonian. During periods of drought, when these water bodies dried out, the fish were left high and dry. Those that could exist out of the water for a while were the ones that survived. Soon there developed fish with lungs to breathe air, and with paired muscular fins to help them to crawl over land. So land-living was developed, enabling fish to survive until the water came back. Soon the first amphibians evolved – animals that only needed to live in the water when they were young, or reproducing. All this happened in Devonian times.

The lush Carboniferous swamps were a haven for all sorts of amphibians. There were huge crocodile-like amphibians that cruised the muddy waterways snapping up fish, and there were agile lizard-like amphibians that scampered over the rotting vegetation, chasing after the myriad insects that lived there. Life in the moist undergrowth was so good and plentiful that the totally land-dwelling reptiles evolved at this time as well.

With the coming of the Permian and the deserts, the plant life developed into more dry land types. There were still the ferns and horsetails of the Carboniferous, but conifers also developed. Land animals also became more adapted to the drier conditions. There were groups of large land-living amphibians, but these still needed to be near the water. The reptiles evolved into many different types. The main thrust of reptile evolution in the Permian was towards the mammal-like reptiles. These began with sail-backed pelycosaurs, with mouths full of different-sized teeth and fins on their backs to help to regulate their temperature. Towards the end of the period the teeth of the mammal-like reptiles were like those of dogs, with killing and holding teeth at the front and meat-shearing teeth at the back. Their temperature control systems were completely internal. Some of the mammal-like reptiles even developed hairy coats.

The other direction of reptile evolution was towards the archosaurs. These tended to be aquatic reptiles, like the crocodiles, who dwelt in swamps and desert streams.

▲ The Devonian landscape (above) was generally one of rugged mountains and desert plains. However, along the banks of the rivers and around the lakes, forests began to grow. These swampy forests became vast in Carboniferous times (right), and gave rise to our coal deposits of today. In the Permian (below) the dry conditions returned and the animal life became adapted to a desert existence.

TRIASSIC GEOGRAPHY

The Triassic period, between 248 and 213 million years ago, was the first period of the Mesozoic era, the first period of the age of dinosaurs.

It was also the age of Pangaea – the supercontinent that was made up of all the continents of the world. The great island that was South-east Asia, and some other local fragments of continents, finally fused with the rest of the continental masses and produced the single vast supercontinent. The rest of the world, covering well over half the globe, was a single ocean – Panthalassa.

The deserts of the Permian continued into the Triassic, but where, in the Permian there were mountain ranges, now there were rounded hills. A huge gulf called the Tethys Sea reached in from the region of China in the east, right through to the area of modern Europe, cutting Pangaea almost in two. Gondwana lay to the south, and the part in the north has been called Laurasia. At each side the island-studded Tethys spread over low-lying areas in shallow seas and lagoons.

Although the parched deserts dominated the interiors of North and South America, much of Africa and nearly all of Europe, particularly those away from the tropics, had quite lush vegetation. Forests existed in what is now Siberia, Germany, Greenland, Virginia and North Carolina, where the climates were cooler.

Towards the end of the period, Pangaea began to tear itself apart once more. Great cracks and rift valleys developed along the line of weakness that would eventually separate South America from Africa. Volcanoes produced vast quantities of hot, runny lava here which built up in vast thicknesses and formed wide plateaux in South Africa.

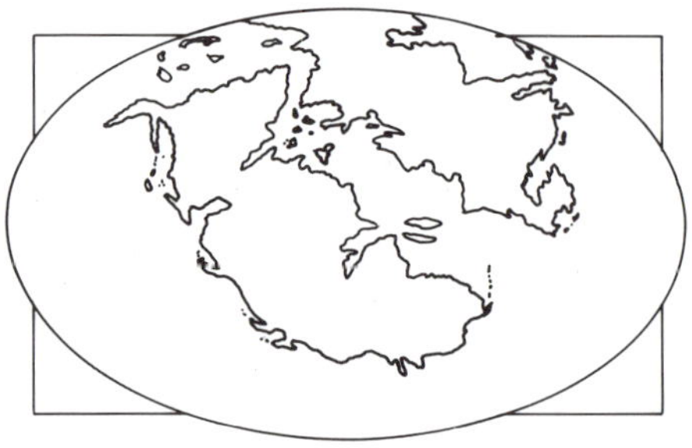

EARLY JURASSIC
180 million years ago

EARLY CRETACEOUS
130 million years ago

▶ The Triassic world as seen from space would have been quite a different place from the one that we know. The main colours on the single great continent of Pangaea would have been the reds, browns, and yellows of desert surface. From the other side, the planet would have been totally blue – the one enormous ocean of Panthalassa would have covered three quarters of the globe. The day would have been slightly shorter in the Triassic. The Earth turned on its axis once every 23 hours then. It has been slowing down ever since.

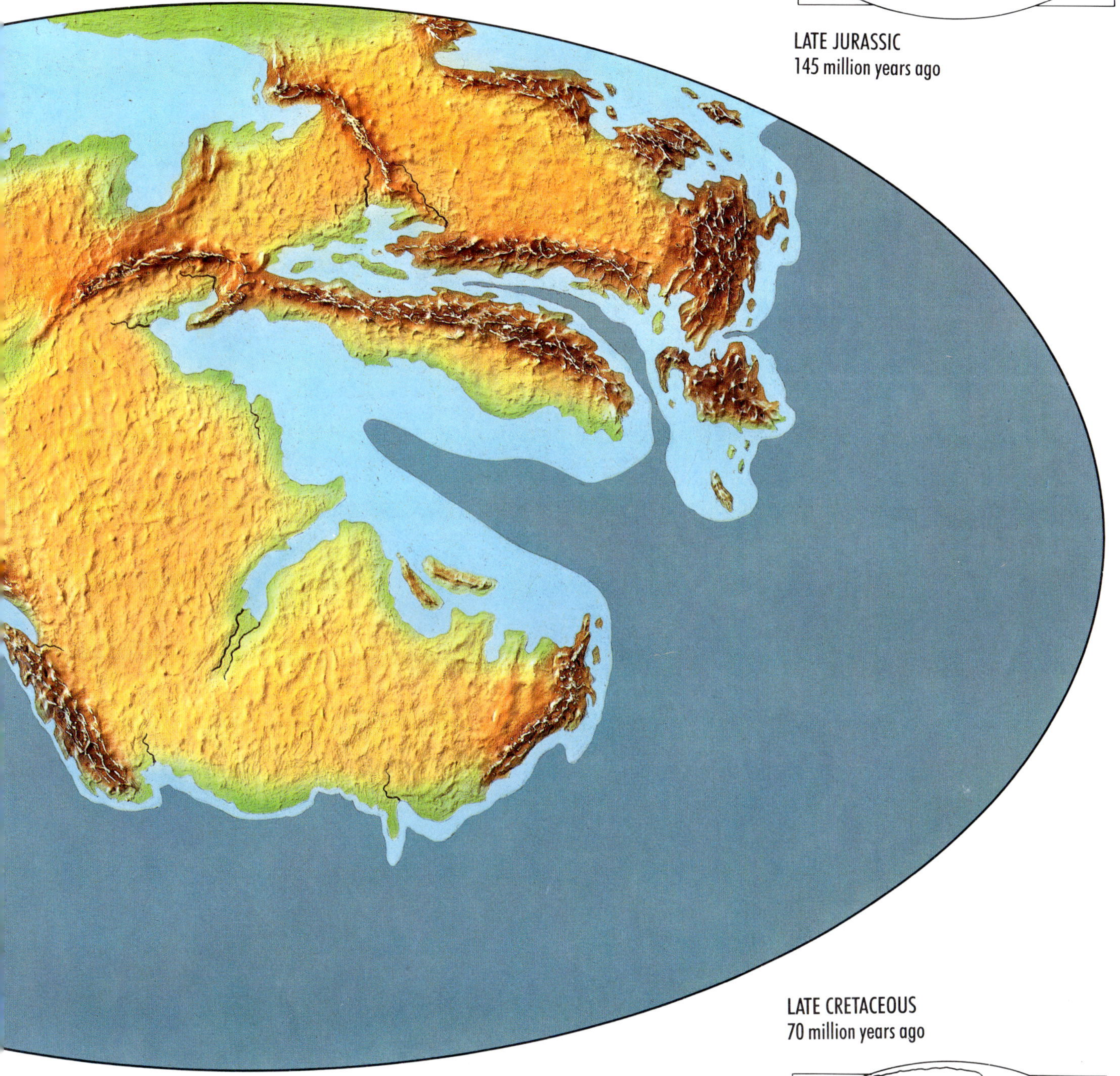

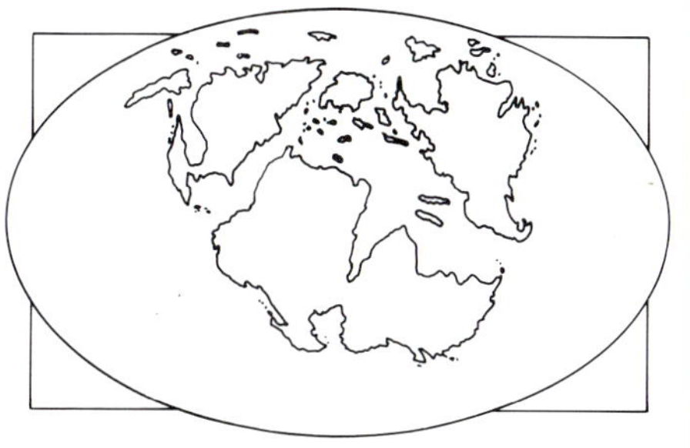

LATE JURASSIC
145 million years ago

LATE CRETACEOUS
70 million years ago

TRIASSIC CONDITIONS

In the far west, the breakers and surf of Panthalassa swept in past chains of volcanic islands and met a mountainous shoreline along the line of the Rocky Mountains and the Andes. Eastward from this edge stretched the vast arid lands of the North American and South American continents. Windswept deserts of shifting sand dunes and rocky outcrops were the main landscapes here, washed by the occasional desert downpour producing deep wadis and temporary oases. The oases in the north consisted of ferns, cycads and conifers clustering around temporary springs and pools. In the south, the vegetation consisted of an extinct group of plants called seed-ferns.

The mammal-like reptiles had begun to decline now, although they were still important amongst the seed-fern meadows of Gondwana. Their descendants, the mammals, had evolved, but these were small, insignificant-looking creatures and were to remain like that for 160 million years.

The archosaurs now came into their own. While they pursued a swimming crocodile-like existence, their hind legs grew long and their tails grew strong. These helped them to swim, but once on land archosaurs evolved that could walk on their long hind legs, balanced by their strong tails. This shape was the basic shape of the most successful archosaur group – the dinosaurs.

The first dinosaurs, including *Coelophysis* (p. 28–9) in North America and *Staurikosaurus* (p. 30–1) in South America, scurried and hunted across the dry landscape. *Anchisaurus* (p. 32–3) also foraged in the North American deserts and oases.

Amongst the limestone islands of the western Tethys, where southern Europe and the Mediterranean now lie, the seas were infested

The arid landscape of Triassic Gondwana was scattered with green, where rivers and lakes provided enough moisture for oases to grow. The plants here were mostly the now-extinct seed ferns. The last of the mammal-like reptiles lived here, including specialized plant-eating types like *Lystrosaurus*. Other reptiles included beak-headed rhynchosaurs, such as *Scaphonyx*. All these were soon to be replaced by the dinosaurs.

with paddle-legged sea reptiles, such as the nothosaurs, and the first plesiosaurs and ichthyosaurs. The earliest pterosaurs – hairy reptiles with wings supported by a long fourth finger – flew around the crags here. Between the fertile edges of the lagoons and the remains of the Variscan hills to the north, herds of dinosaur, like *Plateosaurus* (p. 34–5), migrated. They may have spent the wet season amongst the valleys and gorges of the hills, and travelled across the deserts to pass the dry season foraging along the shores of the Tethys. In the arid limestone plateaux on the northern flanks of the Variscan hills – where England and Wales now lie – there were caves and gorges haunted by lizards, small dinosaurs and tiny mammals. Gliding thecodonts, with wings supported by outstretched ribs, floated, butterfly-like, from pinnacle to dusty pinnacle looking for insects amongst the dry rocks.

◀ Amongst the dry, worn crags of the Laurasian hills lived the small lizard-like desert animals and the first dinosaurs. Flying reptiles, such as *Kuehneosaurus*, glided from dusty outcrop to dusty outcrop.

▼ Life was abundant in the Triassic seas. As well as a multitude of invertebrates, including the first of the coil-shelled ammonites and strange shellfish that built up huge reef structures, there were many kinds of fish and some spectacular sea reptiles. These included the fish-eating *Nothosaurus*, that was very common along the shallows and the beaches of the Tethys, as was the newt-like *Placodus*, with the heavy teeth for picking and crushing shellfish.

COELOPHYSIS BAURI

'BAUR'S HOLLOW FORM'
THEROPODA, COELUROSAUR
LATE TRIASSIC
NORTH AMERICA

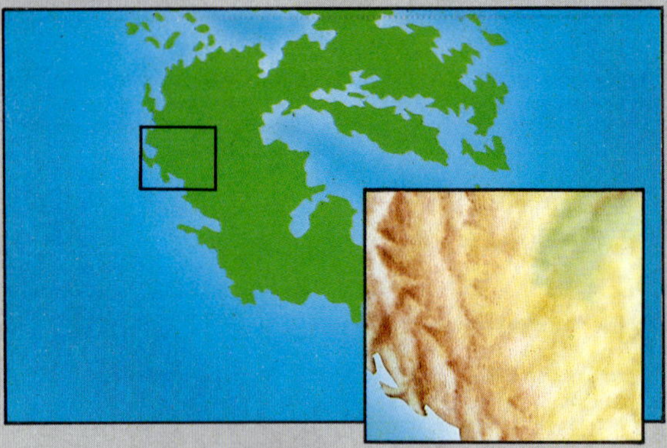

North America was mostly desert at the time, but the hilly regions may have been moist and forested.

Coelophysis was described in 1889 by Edward Drinker Cope from remains first unearthed by amateur fossil collector David Baldwin, in 1881. The species was named 'Baur' after one of the fossil collectors who worked for Cope.

The most important study of the animal was carried out by Edwin H. Colbert in 1947.

A fully grown *Coelophysis* was about 3 metres (10 feet) long. Much of the length was neck and tail, and so it may have weighed only about 30 kilograms (65 pounds).

Coelophysis was carnivorous and may have eaten any small thing that moved, including its own young. It probably hunted in packs.

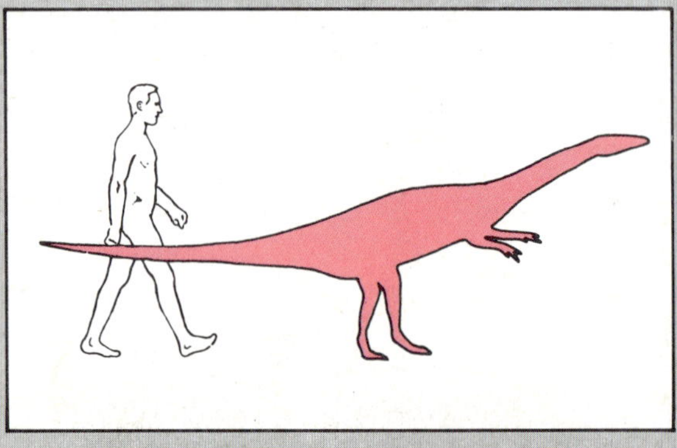

This rather spindly-looking dinosaur with the snaky neck was one of the first to evolve, back in the late Triassic. It looked very much like its ancestors – the lizard-like thecodonts. The main improvement over its predecessors was in the way it stood. The hind legs were held directly beneath the body, like those of a mammal, rather than out at the side as in most reptiles. The head was long, with many saw-edged teeth, and balanced at the end of a slender, flexible neck. The skull was very light and full of holes. These features – the legs held directly beneath the body and the skull full of holes – were present in all the other dinosaurs that later developed.

In the 1880s, when the first discoveries were made, only bits and pieces were found. It was not until 1947 that scientists had a clear idea of what *Coelophysis* actually looked like. In that year a whole graveyard of the beasts' remains was discovered in New Mexico, USA, at a place called Ghost Ranch, not far from where the original bits were found in the 1880s. Dozens of them lay all together, and it is probable that they had been swept away and buried by a sudden flood. Flash floods like this must have been common at the time. The famous Petrified Forest in nearby Arizona is, in fact, a preserved log jam of tree trunks caught in a torrent.

In the body cavities of some of the skeletons there were bones of *Coelophysis* babies. They must have been eaten by the adults.

The teeth were curved and backward pointing – larger in the upper jaw than the lower. The muscles were arranged so that the jaws could be pulled back and forth against one another like the blades of an electric carving-knife.

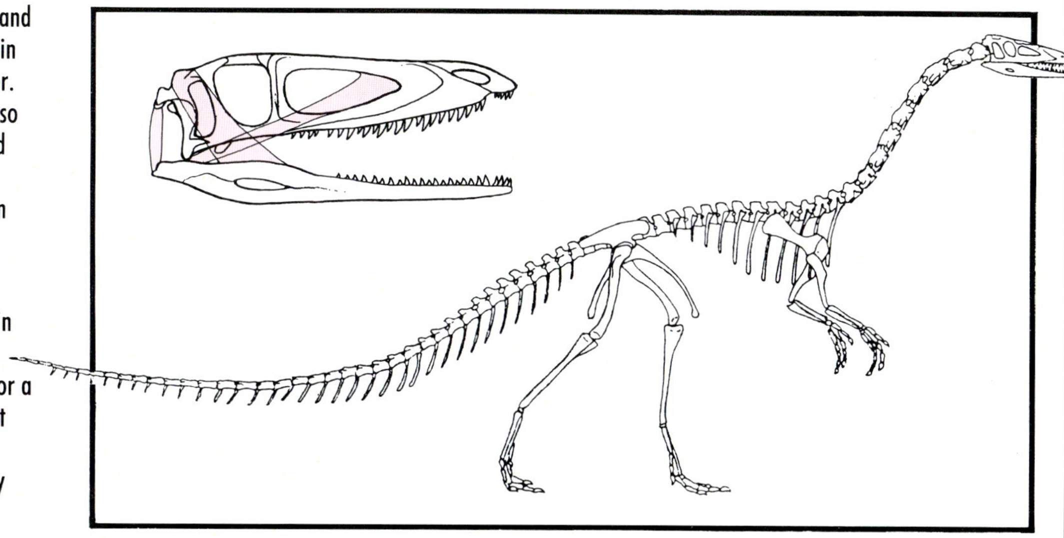

These fossil footprints in sandstone from Connecticut were made by *Coelophysis*, or a dinosaur very much like it. It was once thought that the footprints had been made by ancient birds.

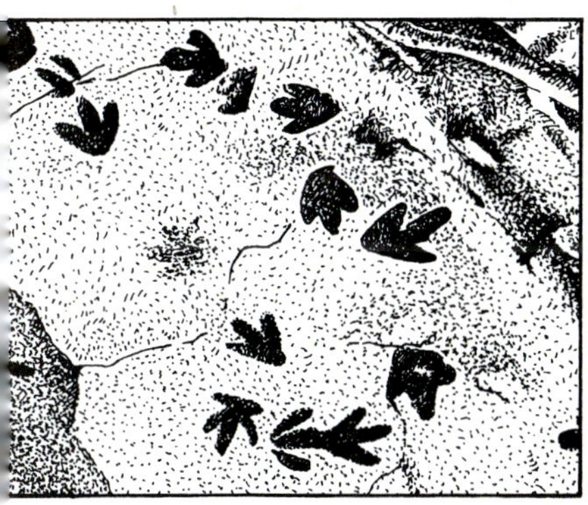

Coelophysis had four fingers on the hand, but only three of these were of any use.

Coelophysis was a fast runner, and probably hunted in packs through upland forests.

STAURIKOSAURUS PRICEI

'LIZARD OF THE SOUTHERN CROSS'
THEROPODA OR SAUROPODOMORPHA, STAURIKOSAURID
MIDDLE TRIASSIC
BRAZIL

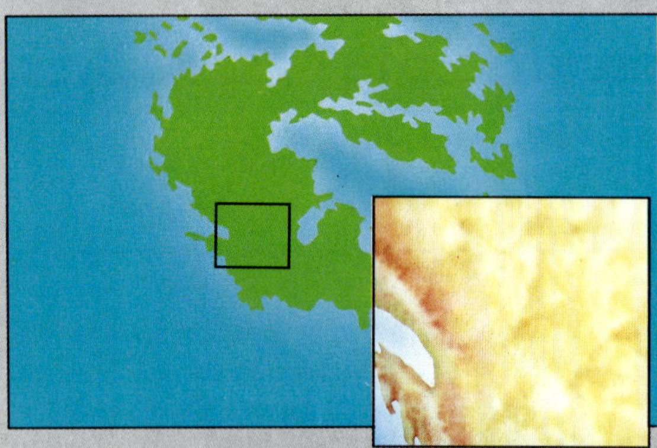

The only specimen of this small, early dinosaur was unearthed in the area of Rio Grande do Sul in southern Brazil.

It was described in 1970 by Edwin H. Colbert of the American Museum of Natural History.

The southern cross of its name refers to the star constellation – the discovery was made when it was unusual to find dinosaurs in the southern hemisphere.

Staurikosaurus must have been about 2 metres (6 feet 6 inches) long. It may have weighed some 30 kilograms (65 pounds).

The teeth were pointed and sharp, so *Staurikosaurus* probably ate meat.

Very little is known about this small animal but it is a very important fossil because, until recently, it was the oldest dinosaur known. In appearance it must have resembled some of the small meat-eating theropods, but some aspects of its skeleton make it more like the plant-eating prosauropods. It is probably close to the point in the evolutionary sequence where these two groups diverged.

However, in 1984, an even older fossil was found in Arizona's Painted Desert, and this looked so much like a prosauropod that it was obvious that the prosauropod group had evolved earlier than *Staurikosaurus*.

Since *Staurikosaurus* is a very early dinosaur, and the pieces of the skeleton we know about are very primitive, we can assume that the missing parts were very primitive as well. Hence, *Staurikosarus* is restored with five toes on its foot and five fingers on its hand – both very primitive and unspecialized features.

▼ The tail was long and slim.

▶ The jawbone suggests that the head was quite large, giving it the appearance of a small version of one of the larger meat-eaters.

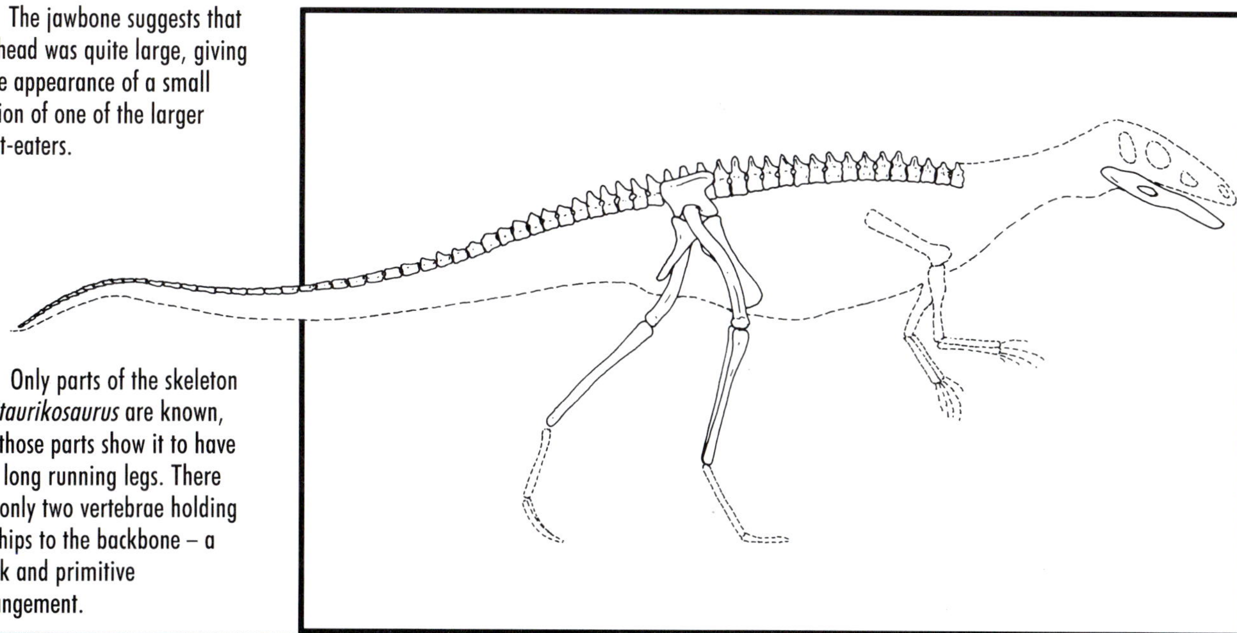

▶ Only parts of the skeleton of *Staurikosaurus* are known, but those parts show it to have had long running legs. There are only two vertebrae holding the hips to the backbone – a weak and primitive arrangement.

ANCHISAURUS POLYZELUS

'NEAR LIZARD'
SAUROPODOMORPHA, PROSAUROPOD
LATE JURASSIC
CONNECTICUT, USA, AND SOUTH AFRICA

The fact that *Anchisaurus* is found both in America and Africa shows that the continents were all together as one great supercontinent at that time.

The first *Anchisaurus* remains were found in 1818. Since nobody knew anything about dinosaurs in those days, it was assumed that the bones were human. Later, more bones were found and by 1855 it was realized that they were reptile bones. The name *Anchisaurus* was given to them by Othniel Charles Marsh in 1885. In 1971, Peter Galton worked on another species, *A. capensis*, discovered in South Africa.

Anchisaurus was quite a small dinosaur – otherwise its bones would not have been mistaken for human bones – and reached a length of just over 2 metres (7 feet). It probably weighed about 27 kilograms (60 pounds).

Anchisaurus was one of the earliest of the plant-eating dinosaurs, although it may have eaten meat as well. Palaeontologists are not very sure about this.

The prosauropods were a group of dinosaurs that enjoyed a brief surge of importance at the end of the Triassic and the beginning of the Jurassic. In appearance they looked like a half-way stage between the two-footed meat-eaters and the four-footed plant-eaters. They probably ate plants for most of the time. Plant-eating needs a much longer gut than meat-eating, as plants are more difficult to digest, and as the prosauropods had the lizard-like hip with the pubis bone pointing forward, the big prosauropod gut had to be carried well forward in the body. This would have made the animal unbalanced when standing on its hind legs, and forced it to take up a four-footed stance.

Anchisaurus was typical of the smaller prosauropods. One very similar prosauropod, unearthed in 1984 and not yet given a name, is the oldest dinosaur skeleton known.

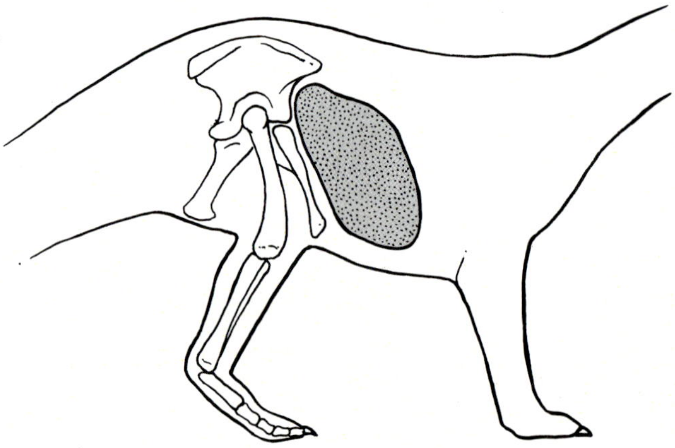

▲ The big gut needed to digest plant food would have forced prosauropods like *Anchisaurus* down on to all fours.

► *Anchisaurus* lived in deserts, probably feeding from plants in oases.

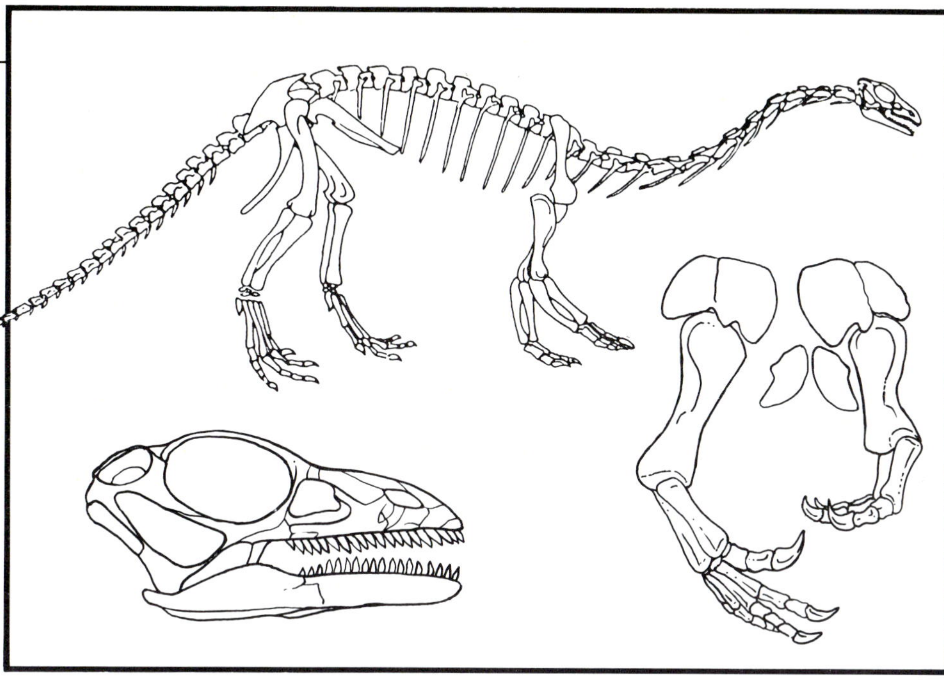

Although many remains of *Anchisaurus* have been found, we still do not have all the bits. Drawings of *Anchisaurus* skeletons have their necks and tails based on those of other prosauropods.

The hand was multi-purpose. When *Anchisaurus* stood on its hind legs the hand could be turned inwards to grasp things. When *Anchisaurus* went on all fours, it could be placed flat against the ground and used as a foot. The first finger could be turned, like a thumb, and had a big claw.

The prosauropods may be at a half-way stage between the two-footed meat-eating theropods, and the huge four-footed plant-eating sauropods.

The head has blunt teeth with file-like edges. These, and the type of jaw hinge, suggest that *Anchisaurus* ate mostly plants.

PLATEOSAURUS ENGELHARDTI

'ENGELHARDT'S FLAT REPTILE'
SAUROPODOMORPHA, PROSAUROPOD
LATE TRIASSIC
FRANCE AND GERMANY

The first *Plateosaurus* was described in 1837 by Hermann von Meyer, from pieces of a skeleton. The best finds were made in Germany between 1911 and 1932 when many complete skeletons were found together.

Plateosaurus was a large prosauropod, reaching a length of 8 metres (26 feet).

As with all later long-necked large dinosaurs, *Plateosaurus* ate plants. It probably swallowed stones to help it grind up plant food in its stomach.

To have watched a *Plateosaurus* walking on all fours we would have been convinced that the animal was close to the ancestors of the big long-necked plant-eaters to come. Indeed, some of its even larger relatives, such as *Riojasaurus*, were so big – 11 metres (36 feet) long – that they were almost the size of the sauropods.

Plateosaurus remains have been found in large numbers all over Europe. Whole graveyards of the beast have been found in the sandstones of Germany and France. This had led to the suggestion that *Plateosaurus* roamed the Triassic deserts in herds. They could have migrated seasonally across the desert, between the fertile shores of the Tethys Sea in the south and the well-watered uplands to the north. Occasionally, an entire herd could have been caught and buried by a sandstorm.

Another explanation for the mass grave may be that they lived in the moist highlands around the desert plains. A dead *Plateosaurus* that had fallen into a stream would have been washed down to the desert and dumped where the water soaked away into the sand. Other bodies would have been dumped in the same place over a period of time, giving the impression that a whole herd had died in the one spot.

▶ *Plateosaurus* may have wandered across the late Triassic deserts in herds, or it may have lived in the hills surrounding the desert plains.

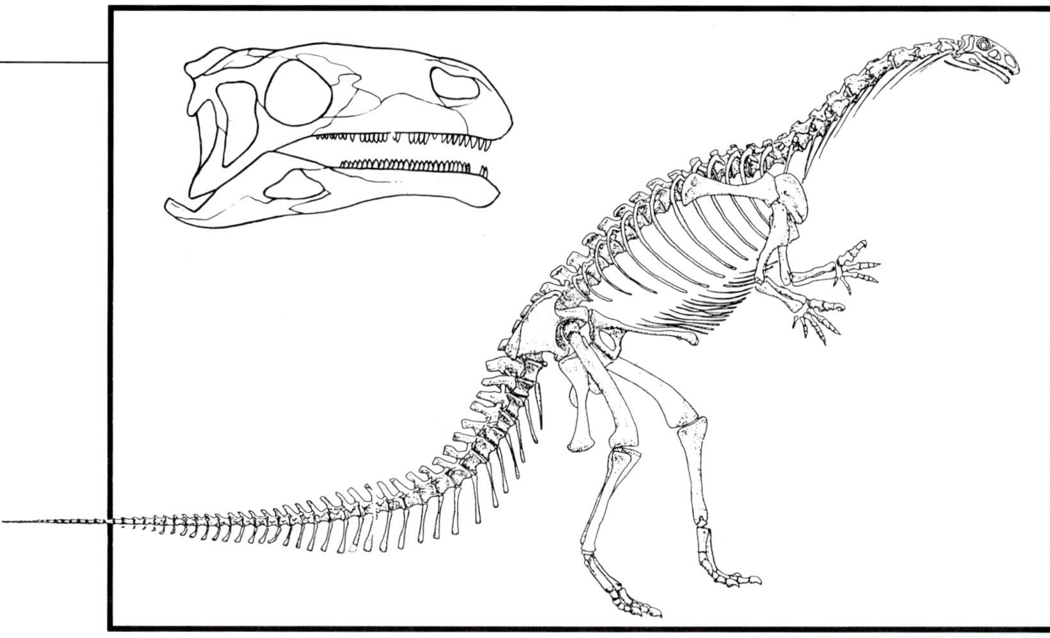

Plateosaurus remains are so common and well known that the skeleton is used as the basis for the shape of all other prosauropods.

The skull has many small teeth compared with those of the smaller prosauropods.

EARLY JURASSIC GEOGRAPHY

The sea swept over the lower-lying fringes of Pangaea in early Jurassic times, about 213 million years ago, and throughout the period these shallow seas came and went. Dry land became flooded and then became dry again. Shallow seas became deep seas, and returned to shallow seas – and became dry land again. All the desert areas of Europe became sea, and the remains of the Variscan hills were strings of low islands across the shallow waters. The seas swept over Northern Canada and Greenland, and swept back again. Over in the east the shallow seas covered north-eastern Siberia, but they withdrew from China, Indonesia and Malaysia, leaving this corner of Pangaea high and dry for most of the rest of the Mesozoic.

Pangaea did still exist at this time but it was beginning to crack up. Rift valleys began to appear along the line that would eventually split North America from Africa and Europe, and narrow seas, like the modern Red Sea, began to reach along them from the north-east, past Greenland, and from the south-west, from the region of today's Gulf of Mexico.

The fold mountain belts and volcanic island chains continued to rise and combine with one another along the west coasts of North and South America. Sometimes, the waters of Panthalassa would break in and sweep past them into the areas of the Gulf of Mexico and Patagonia. More often, the mountains acted as a barrier, keeping the vast ocean away from the continental interiors, as they do today.

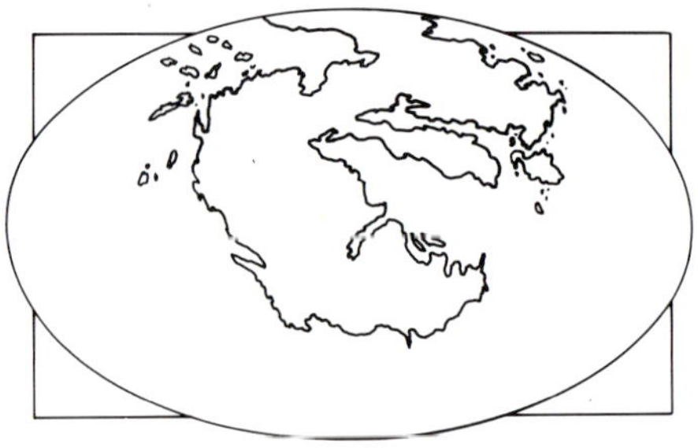

TRIASSIC
215 million years ago

EARLY CRETACEOUS
130 million years ago

Lower Jurassic times represented the last days of Pangaea. Although the single supercontinent was still in existence, it was becoming very unstable and beginning to crack up, rift valleys and volcanic belts reaching in curving lines across the land area. The climate was becoming much less harsh. The dry redness of the continents was giving way to a luxuriant green as shallow waters came and went many times over the low-lying areas. This brought moist conditions to regions that had been desert up to then.

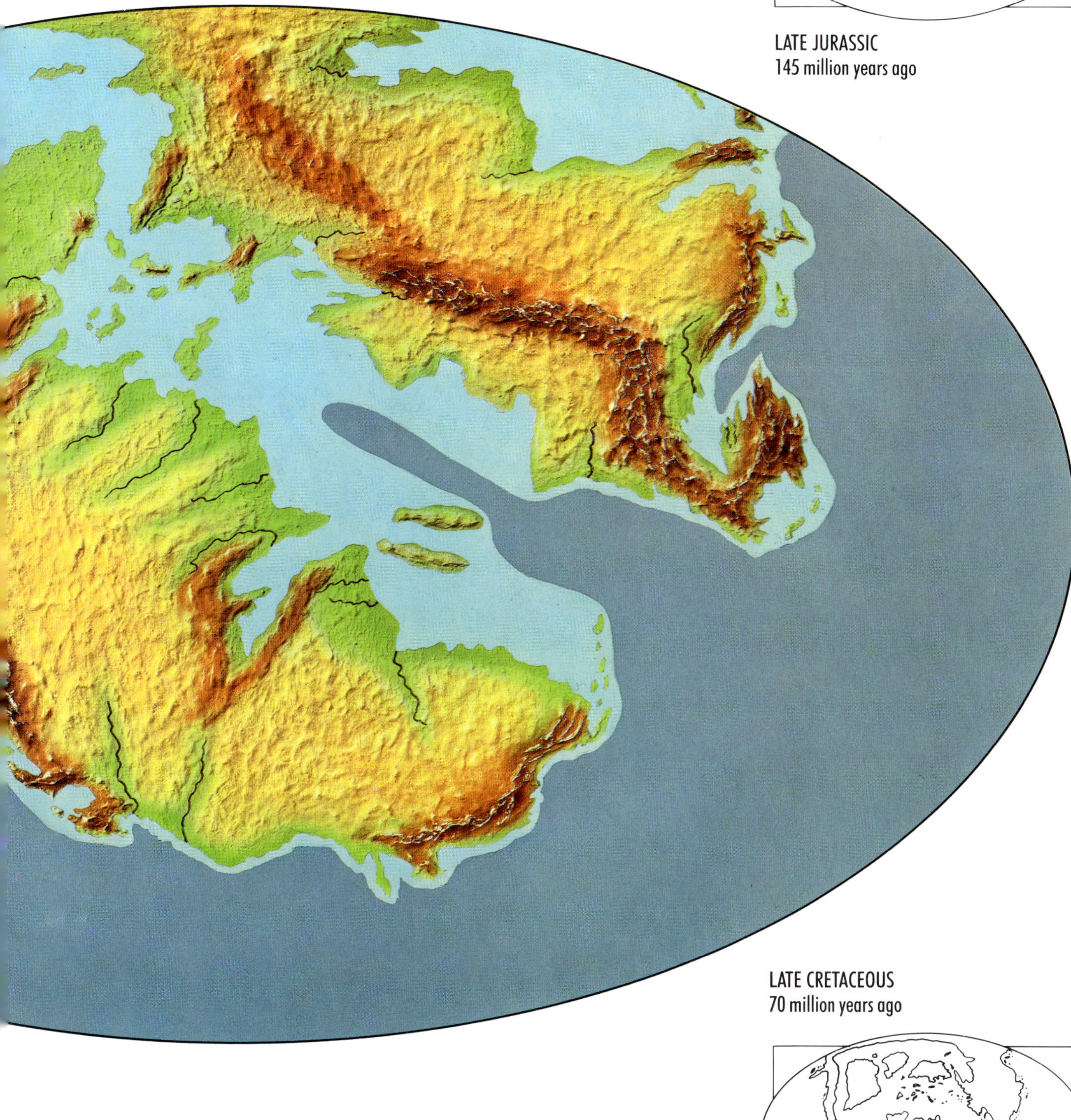

LATE JURASSIC
145 million years ago

LATE CRETACEOUS
70 million years ago

EARLY JURASSIC CONDITIONS

▲ Sea flooded across the low-lying lands of early Jurassic northern Europe, bringing moist climates to continents that had been deserts up until then. Luxuriant forests of ferns, tree ferns and conifers flourished, producing enough vegetation to support large plant-eating dinosaurs. Pterosaurs, such as the insect-eating *Dimorphodon*, flew amongst the trees.

The weather improved in early Jurassic times. When the water spread into the lowland areas it brought moist climates with it to replace the hot dryness of the deserts. Now there were coastlines clothed with green vegetation, and there were deltas and swamps on the lowland areas that were not immersed in the sea.

However, deep in the interiors of the continents, the dry desert conditions hung on for some time. Inland North America was still arid, and the dinosaurs there, such as *Scutellosaurus* (p. 44–5) and *Dilophosaurus* (p. 40–1), had to put up with a dry and dusty climate. Likewise, in southern Africa we find dinosaurs such as *Heterodontosaurus* (p. 46–7) fossilized where they had died waiting vainly in a burrow for the hot dry season to pass.

Elsewhere, conditions were more pleasant. Not far from the dry interior of southern Africa lay the continent of India – part of Gondwana as well. Forests existed here and the plant life was luxurious enough to feed huge plant-eating dinosaurs, like *Barapasaurus* (p. 42–3). Forests also clothed the islands and coastlines of Europe – forests of familiar conifers and ginkgoes (trees with fan-shaped leaves and yellow flowers), interspersed with less familiar cycad-like trees, growing from an undergrowth of horsetails and ferns. *Scelidosaurus* (p. 48–9) browsed amongst these while pterosaurs, such as *Dimorphodon*, swung low overhead catching insects on the wing.

And in the shallow seas? The waters were generally warmer than they are now. Coral reefs formed in the clear water of Europe and in Australia. All kinds of strange invertebrates swam there and have been preserved as fossils. Most notable are the ammonites – relatives of the octopus and cuttlefish encased in a coiled

Some areas of the Earth's surface were still far from the sea and, as a result, were still deserts. The central area of North America was such a place. The oceans were too far away to have any effect on the climate and, as today, the mountains in the west stood between the continent and the nearest ocean. These mountains trapped the moisture from the wet winds from the Panthalassa, and only dry air carried on into the continental interior.

shell – and the belemnites – squid-like in a shell shaped like a bullet. These, and the vast shoals of fish, were preyed upon by the marine reptiles of the time. Crocodiles were so well adapted to sea life they developed flippers instead of feet, and fish-like tails. There were short-headed and long-necked plesiosaurs, such as *Cryptocleidus*, and the pliosaurs with the long heads and short necks, such as *Macroplata*. Probably the best adapted sea reptiles were the dolphin-shaped ichthyosaurs, such as *Leptopterygius*.

The shallow seas were full of life. The ammonites became so abundant and evolved so rapidly that the fossils of different species can now be used to identify the individual beds of Jurassic rocks. Sea reptiles included plesiosaurs, like *Crytocleidus*, ichthyosaurs, like *Leptopterygius* and paddle-limbed sea crocodiles, like *Metriorhynchus*.

DILOPHOSAURUS WETHERILLI

'WETHERILL'S TWO RIDGED LIZARD'
THEROPODA, MEGALOSAURID
EARLY JURASSIC
ARIZONA, USA

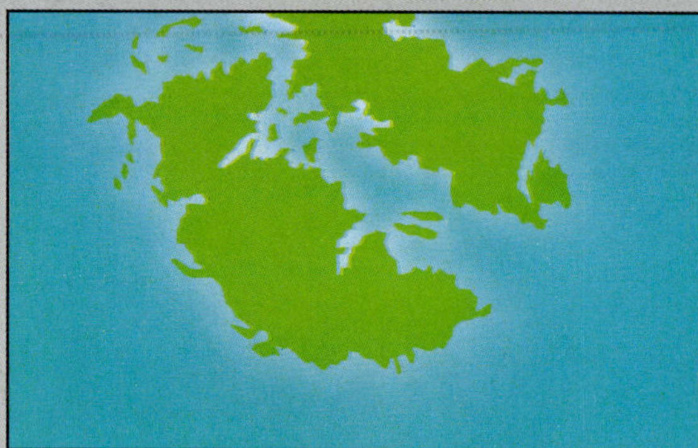

Three skeletons of *Dilophosaurus* were found in an expedition to northern Arizona by the University of California in 1942. The species was described by Samuel Welles in 1954, but was thought to be be a species of *Megalosaurus*. Welles revised his opinion in 1970, when he found a more complete skeleton. He published a more up-to-date account in 1984.

For a megalosaur (see page 78–9), *Dilophosaurus* was quite lightly built. So much so, in fact, that some palaeontologists think it was a very large type of coelurosaurid. The jaws were quite slender, almost crocodile-like, and had a set of very thin and pointed teeth in a separate bunch at the front. Its hands, however, were quite large and it is likely that these were used for killing and dismembering prey – the jaws being rather delicate for this work.

The most peculiar thing about the skeleton found in 1970 was the pair of bony crests on the skull. It was the absence of these from the original skeletons that caused the initial confusion about the identification.

The crests were thin and semicircular, and probably ran from the front to the back of the skull. A short, bony prong stuck out at the rear. No one knows what these crests were for, but it is possible that they were some sort of display structure, and that only the males had them.

Dilophosaurus was one of the earliest of the big meat-eaters.

Dilophosaurus grew to a length of 5.8 metres (20 feet).

Its crocodile-like jaws were obviously for eating meat.

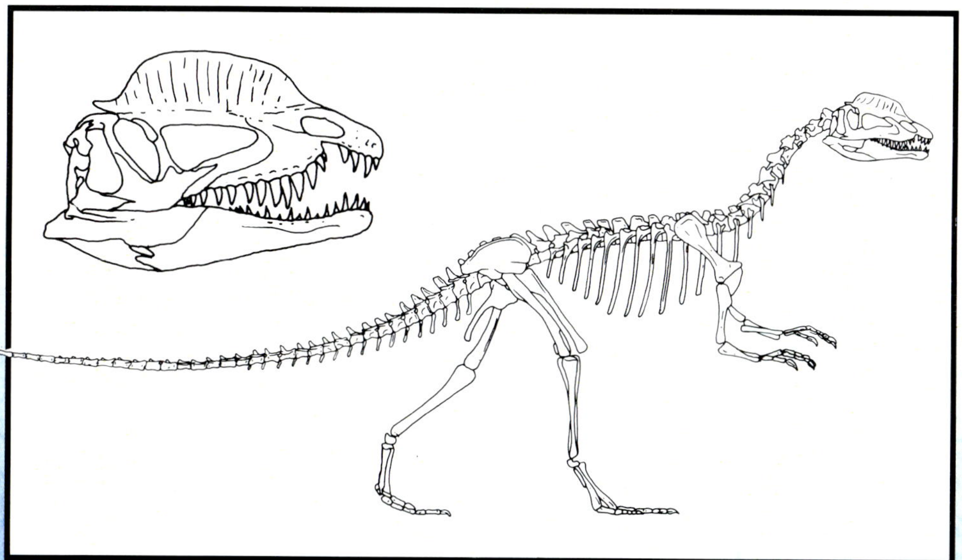

◀ Despite the size, the slender legs and tail and the flexible neck make *Dilophosaurus* look like one of the small coelurosaurs.

▼ The jaws, with the set of sharp teeth at the tip, looked a bit like those of a crocodile. The crests, although not found actually attached to the skull, probably ran parallel to one another along the top.

▼ *Dilophosaurus* must have been the largest flesh-eater of its day.

BARAPASAURUS TAGORSI

'BIG LEGGED LIZARD'
SAUROPODOMORPHA, SAUROPOD
EARLY JURASSIC
INDIA

Bones of *Barapasaurus* were first discovered in 1960, but it was not until 1975 that the species was described. The description was published by Jain, Kutty, Roy-Chowdhury and Chatterjee of Calcutta.

Barapasaurus is the earliest sauropod known, but even at this early stage in sauropod evolution they had reached respectable lengths. *Barapasaurus* was 14 metres (34 feet) long.

Barapasaurus was a plant-eater, but since no skull has been found, it is unclear what exactly it ate.

This was the earliest known of the sauropods – and a very primitive one it was too. Most of the later sauropods were specialized in one form or another. The tall ones, such as *Brachiosaurus* (p. 64–5), had towering necks and high shoulders to allow them to reach up into high trees. The long ones, like *Diplodocus* (p. 66–7), were balanced at the hips by strong tail muscles so that they could reach upwards by lifting their forelegs off the ground. *Barapasaurus* had neither of these specializations. They had quite solid backbones with only the suggestion of hollows. Later sauropods, however, had their backbones hollowed out to become mere frameworks – a weight-saving measure.

From a geographical point of view, this dinosaur is important because it is similar to other early sauropods found in East Africa. At the time at which it lived, India must still have been joined to Africa. It did not break away and move toward its present position until later.

▶ Many bones of *Barapasaurus* have been found, but unfortunately the skull is still a mystery.

▶ Some of the bones were quite similar to those of the prosauropods, but the legs were definitely those of a sauropod. The vertebrae were hollowed out for lightness, but not to such an extent as in the later sauropods.

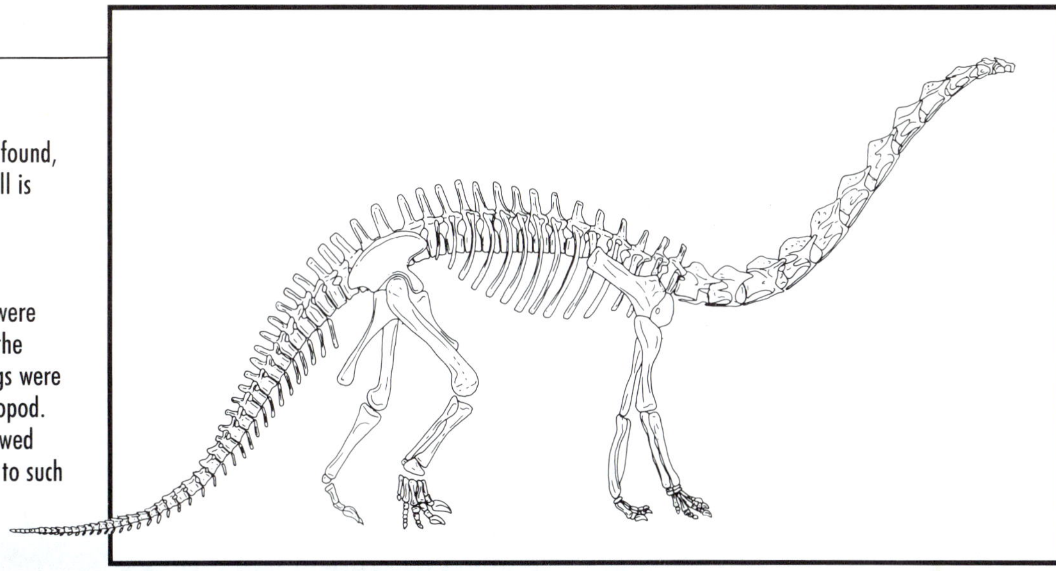

▲ *Barapasaurus* was a tall-backed sauropod with rather long and thin legs.

SCUTELLOSAURUS LAWLERI

'LAWLER'S LIZARD WITH LITTLE SHIELDS'
ORNITHOPODA, FABROSAURID
LATE TRIASSIC OR EARLY JURASSIC
ARIZONA, USA

Scutellosaurus was first described in 1981 by Professor Edwin H. Colbert.

It was quite a small animal, barely reaching a length of 1.2 metres (4 feet), and most of this length was tail.

A plant-eater, *Scutellosaurus* had simple leaf-life teeth, a bit like those of the modern-day iguana lizard. It evidently ate plant material, just as the iguana does.

Imagine a medium-sized lizard, covered in spiky knobs like a horned toad, scampering about on the dry plains of lower Jurassic North America. This is how *Scutellosaurus* would have appeared. However, while a modern-day lizard would be running about with its belly close to the ground and its legs flailing out at the side, *Scutellosaurus* would be running with its legs held beneath it, like a small mammal. To get out of our way it may have lifted its forelimbs clear of the ground and run on its hind legs, with its body balanced at the hips by its long, swinging tail. Then, in a cleft in the rocks it may have stopped to defend itself – pressing its body close to the ground and presenting only its armoured back towards us.

The fabrosaurids, of which *Scutellosaurus* is the only known American example, were the most primitive of the bird-footed bird-hipped dinosaurs. These all had the swept-back hip structure and the toothless bone in the front of the jaw. However, the fabrosaurid face would have been very lizard-like compared with the other bird-hipped dinosaurs. It had not developed the muscular cheek-pouches that they had, and so it would have torn at its food and swallowed it in unchewed mouthfuls, like modern plant-eating iguanas do.

▼ Fabrosaurids probably slept right through the hot summer months in burrows, only coming out when the wet season rains produced enough vegetation.

This skull is of *Lesothosaurus*, a closely-related southern African fabrosaurid. The teeth are simple and leaf-shaped, and there is no room for cheek-pouches.

The complete skull of *Scutellosaurus* has not been found – only the lower jaw.

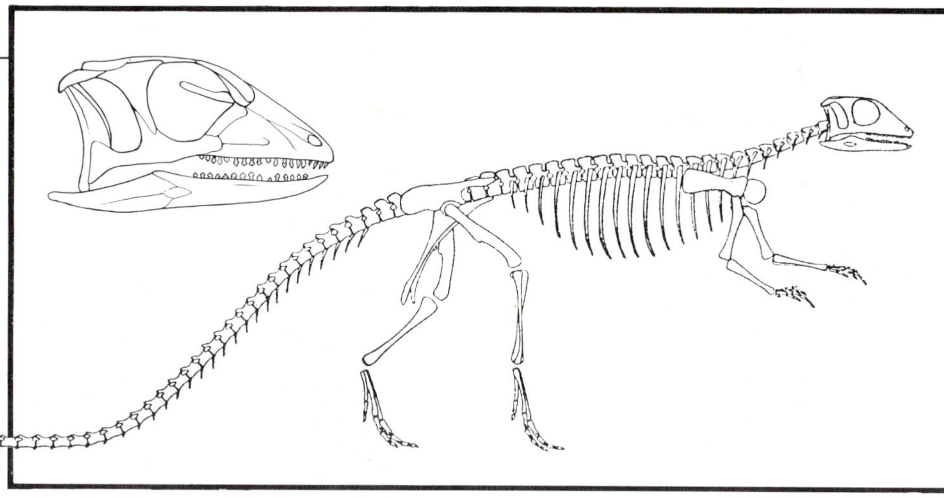

The skelton differs from that of other fabrosaurids in having the bony armour.

Other fabrosaurids, such as *Lesothosaurus*, did not rely on armour for defence. They ran away on two legs. Their very short forelimbs show this.

HETERODONTOSAURUS TUCKI

'TUCK'S LIZARD WITH THE VARIED TEETH'
ORNITHOPODA, HETERODONTOSAURID
LATE TRIASSIC OR EARLY JURASSIC
SOUTH AFRICA

The first heterodontosaurid fossil, a piece of jaw bone, was discovered in 1911, but it was not clear what kind of animal it had belonged to. Another skeleton of *Heterodontosaurus* was discovered in 1962, by Dr Alan Charig, Dr John Attridge and Dr Barry Cox, and by 1976, when a complete skeleton was found, the details of the creature were clear.

Its length was 85 centimetres (about 2 feet 8 inches).

Despite the long canine teeth, like those of a dog, *Heterodontosaurus* was a plant-eater.

It is little wonder that the palaeontologists who found the first jawbone were unsure about the kind of animal to which it belonged. The different kinds of teeth in the one jaw suggested that it must have been some sort of mammal. There was a horny beak on the lower jaw – something all bird-hipped dinosaurs posessed. This would have made contact with a bony pad on the upper jaw. At each side of this bony upper pad were small, sharp gripping teeth. Then came the tusks, in the position of a dog's pointed killing teeth. At the back was a set of shearing teeth that would have worked along with cheek pouches to enable the animal to chew its plant food throughly.

Heterodontosaurus was a lightly-built running dinosaur, as shown by the bones of the hind legs, and there was a series of stiffening rods that kept the lower part of the back and the base of the tail quite straight. This was much better developed in later bird-hipped dinosaurs.

A skull of *Heterodontosaurus* has been found which lacks the tusks. At first, it was thought to belong to a different species of *Heterodontosaurus*, and was given the scientific name *H. consors*. However, scientists now think that it belonged to a female of the same species, and that the tusks were used by the males in some form of mating display.

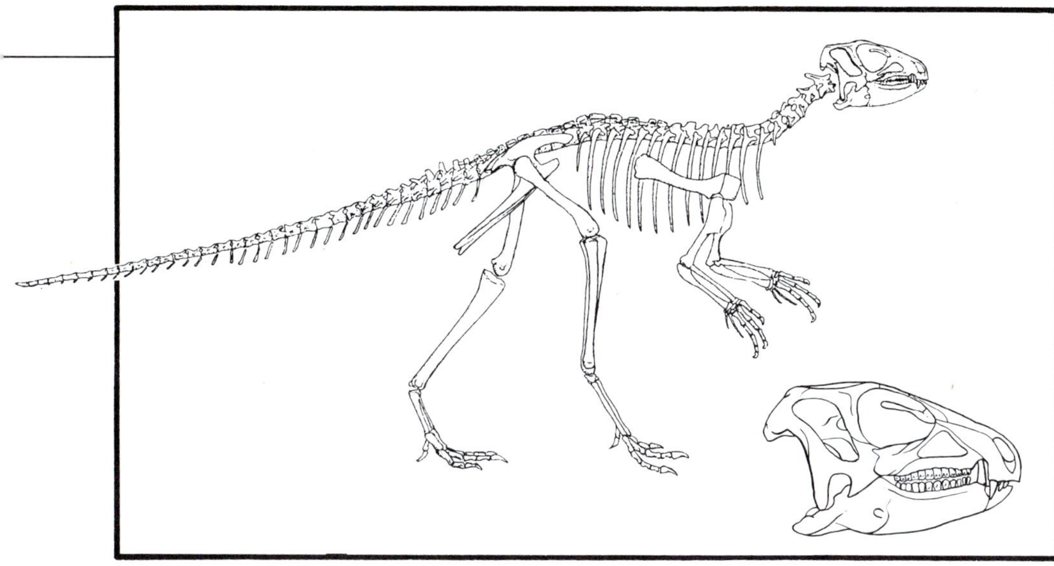

The large hand with the five fingers may have been used for digging for food.

The hollows in the side of the skull show where the cheek pouches were.

The hind legs of *Heterodontosaurus* had short thighs, and long shins and foot bones. This is a distinctive feature of a running animal – where all the leg muscle is concentrated near the hips.

It is rare to find a fossil in better condition than this complete *Heterodontosaurus* skeleton.

The males may have used the tusks in a mating display.

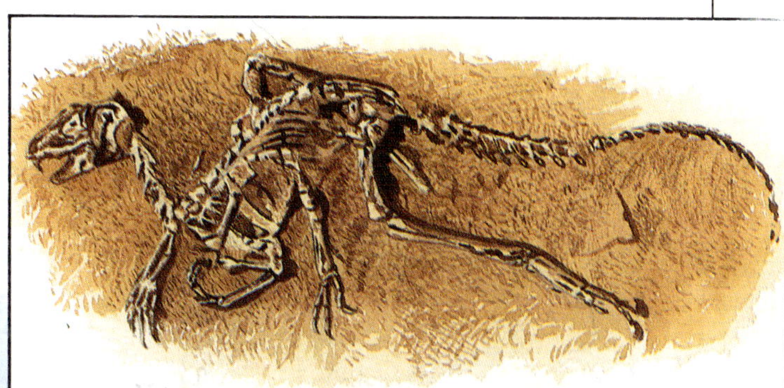

SCELIDOSAURUS HARRISONI

'HARRISON'S LIMB REPITLE'
ANKYLOSAURIA, SCELIDOSAURID
EARLY JURASSIC
SOUTHERN ENGLAND, WITH A CLOSE RELATIVE IN PORTUGAL

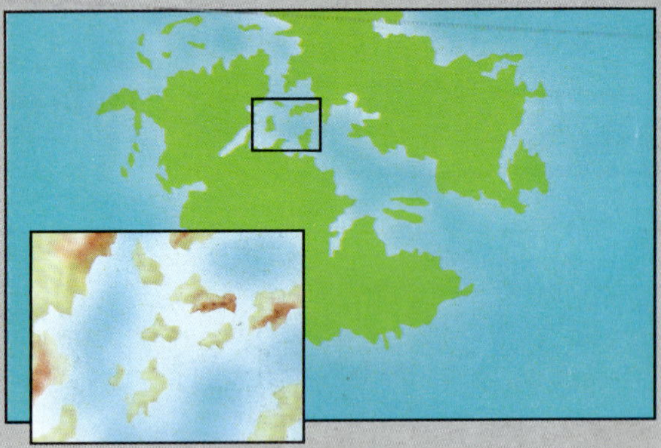

Some pieces found by a physician, Dr J. Harrison, were named *Scelidosaurus* by Richard Owen in 1861. He went on to describe an almost complete skeleton in 1863. Since then, Harrison's original bones were found to have belonged to another creature altogther, but the name stuck with the complete skeleton. No other remains were found until 1980, and then, in 1985, some good fossils were uncovered in Dorset, England, by amateur collectors David Costain, Peter Langham and Simon Barnsley.

Owen's original skeleton remained in its block of stone in the British Museum (Natural History) for over a century. In 1985, work was begun to remove the bones from the rock in which it was embedded.

Scelidosaurus was 3.5 metres (11 feet) long.

It had small conical teeth at the front of the jaw and flat leaf-like teeth at the back. It was a plant-eater, as were all the other armoured dinosaurs.

Scelidosaurus probably ate ferns and the palmtree-like cycads.

The bony armour was less developed than that of the later ankylosaurs.

Scelidosaurus, the oldest known armoured dinosaur, was a very primitive beast. It was a lumbering, four-footed creature with rows of bony plates and spikes down its back. The plates and spikes looked a little like those of the ancestral thecodonts. The hip bone also was very primitive. However, these features – the rows of plates and the primitive hip bone – are found in the later ankylosaurs, and so we can assume that *Scelidosaurus*, or something very similar, was the ankylosaurs' ancestor. The small leaf-like teeth and the arrangement of the bones of the skull into a rigid box-like structure are also ankylosaurian features.

Scelidosaurus lived on the wooded islands scattered across the shallow sea that lay over northern Europe in lower Jurassic times. The bodies may occasionally have been washed out to sea where they sank into the mud, to be found millions of years later in the marine sedimentary rocks.

No reconstruction of the skeleton has yet been made. The original skeleton remained in its block of rock until the mid 1980s.

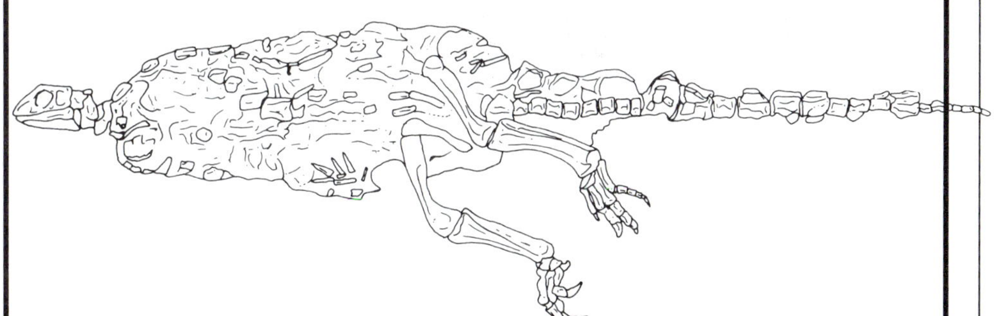

In the hips, the pubis bone lies flat back against the ischium bone as in all other bird-hipped dinosaurs. However, there is no forward pointing tongue at the top. Although this is a primitive feature, the later ankylosaurs also show this.

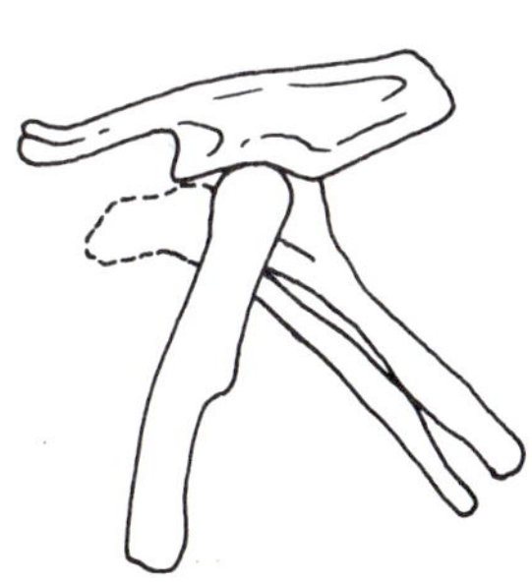

LATE JURASSIC GEOGRAPHY

Now, in the second half of the Jurassic, between about 180 and 144 million years ago, Pangaea started ripping itself apart in earnest. North America began to rotate clockwise and, in doing so, tore itself away from Africa. It was still joined to northern Europe, however, but since the area of the join was almost continuously covered by shallow sea there was no dry land connection between the land masses. It would have been possible to take a boat from the Tethys, through the waterway between the islands of Europe and up to the North Pole, or from the Tethys down through the opening ocean between North America and Africa to the Gulf of Mexico and out through the volcanic island chains of Central America and into the tumultuous waters of Panthalassa. This would have been a hazardous journey, however, since you would have been carried onwards uncontrollably by a westward-flowing current that would have swept round between the continents and out across the ocean.

Shallow seas reached deep into the interiors of the continents. The young Rocky Mountains formed a long rugged peninsula at the time, as an arm of sea, called the Sundance Sea, spread southwards across much of western North America. Europe was again mostly shallow sea, but with wooded islands dotted here and there. Scandinavia was a high land mass of granite moorland. The Ural Mountains formed a string of islands, and beyond these a shallow sea called the Ob Basin spread over much of Siberia.

On the southern shores of the Tethys an arm of shallow sea reached deep into the heart of Gondwana, along the line of the rift that was to separate India and Madagascar from the mainland of Africa. Rift valleys were already forming between southern Africa and Antarctica, and these were regions of long, steep-sided valleys and volcanoes.

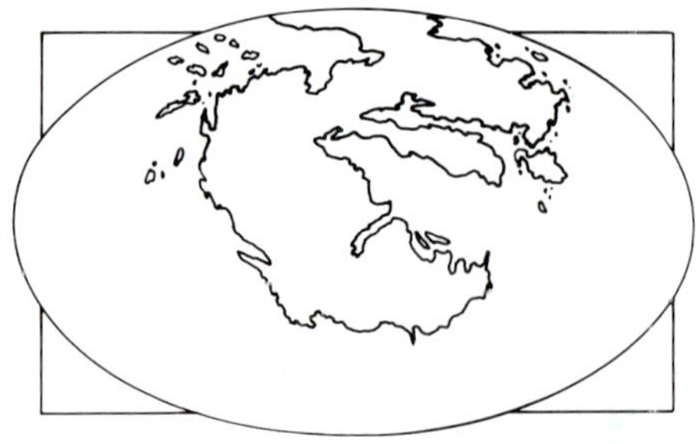

TRIASSIC
215 million years ago

▶ Pangaea was now coming apart, with North America twisting away from Africa and Europe and the Atlantic ocean beginning to grow in between. Gondwana was still one solid piece of supercontinent, although it was beginning to weaken as well. Three quarters of the globe was still covered by the one great ocean Panthalassa, and the Tethys was still present as a huge gulf reaching in from the east. Shallow seas continued to spread over lowland continents, particularly in Europe and western Asia, and the climate remained warm, moist and stable.

EARLY CRETACEOUS
130 million years ago

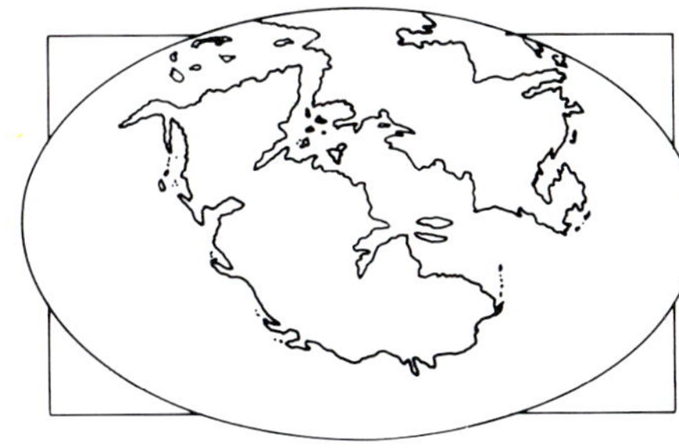

EARLY JURASSIC
180 million years ago

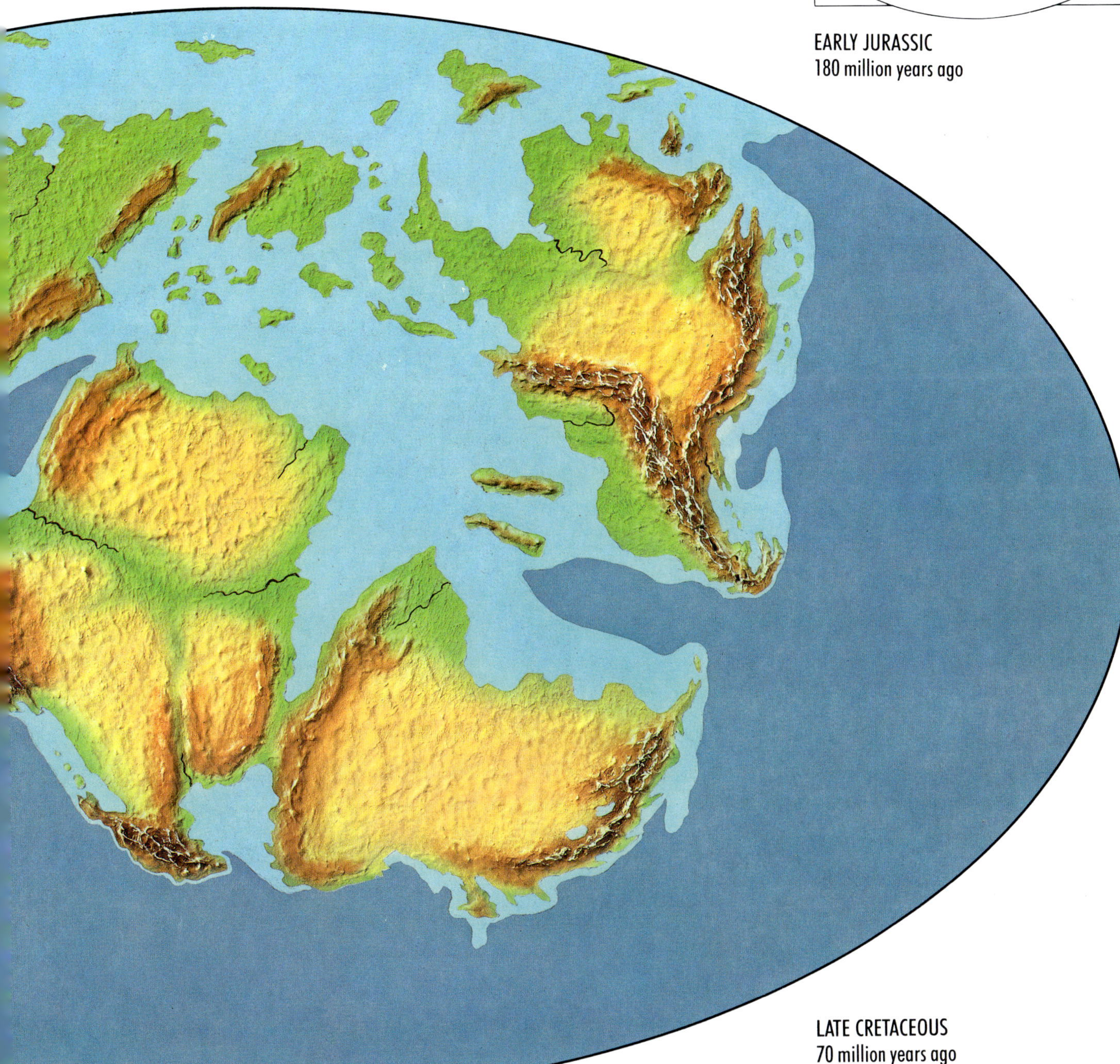

LATE CRETACEOUS
70 million years ago

LATE JURASSIC CONDITIONS

The warm, moderate climates continued through the late Jurassic. Forests and open plains of ferns grew everywhere. Frequent rainfall washed the slopes of the young Rocky Mountains and sand and silt was washed down to the lowlands bordering the Sundance Sea. There they spread out in deltas and mud-banks that became colonized by plants – conifers, cycads and ginkgoes again – and formed a broad fertile floodplain. The sedimentary rocks formed by all the sand, silt and gravel are now found in a belt stretching from Montana to New Mexico, USA, and known as the Morrison Formation. Some of the most well-known dinosaurs of the time lived on these plains, including the plant-eaters *Camarasaurus*, (p. 62–3) *Diplodocus* (p. 66–7) and *Stegosaurus* (p. 70–1), and the meat-eaters *Ornitholestes* (p. 56–7), *Ceratosaurus* (p. 58–9) and *Allosaurus* (p. 60–1). Crocodiles hunted in the shallow waters, and pterosaurs flew overhead.

Almost the same conditions existed in East Africa, where rivers flowed eastward to the arm of the sea that stretched south from the Tethys.

▲ Between the Rocky Mountains and the shores of the inland Sundance sea in North America there was a region of low-lying wooded river plains. This gave rise to the famous Morrison Formation – one of the world's most dinosaur-rich sequences of rocks.

There, sandbanks prevented the rivers from draining directly into the sea, and swamps and plains were built up. There lived similar types of dinosaurs as in North America, including *Brachiosaurus* (p. 64–5) and *Kentrosaurus* (p. 72–3).

The same kind of animals also existed in China, where the same conditions prevailed. Dinosaurs like *Mamenchisaurus* (p. 68–9) and the stegosaur *Tuojiangosaurus* lived here.

The quiet lagoons and bays between the islands of Europe gave rise to some very fine-grained limestones, with beautifully preserved skeletons of animals that had fallen into the still waters. These include the dinosaur *Compsognathus* (p. 54–5) as well as the pterosaurs *Pterodactylus* and *Rhamphorhynchus*, and also the first bird – a little creature like a dinosaur covered in feathers, called *Archaeopteryx*.

Sea life was just as spectacular as it was in the early Jurassic, with the plesiosaurs and ichthyosaurs as common as they ever were. The toothless *Opthalmosaurus* from European waters was probably the most streamlined ichthyosaur that ever lived.

◄ In East Africa, wooded river plains supported the same kind of dinosaur fauna as is found in the Morrison Formation. This shows that the same animal types existed over very large areas of the globe. With the break-up of Pangaea, the late Jurassic was probably the last time this could have happened.

▼ Wooded islands with sheltered lagoons lay scattered over the shallow seas of northern Europe. The smallest dinosaurs lived here. Flying creatures abounded, including primitive, long-tailed pterosaurs like *Rhamphorhynchus*, more advanced short-tailed types like *Pterodactylus*, and the first bird, *Archaeopteryx*.

COMPSOGNATHUS LONGIPES

'PRETTY JAW WITH LONG LEGS'

THEROPODA, COELUROSAUR

LATE JURASSIC

GERMANY AND FRANCE

Wooded islands in the shallow European sea were the home of *Compsognathus.*

The first specimen of *Compsognathus* was unearthed by amateur fossil collector Dr Oberndorfer, fossilized in the fine limestone, called lithographic limestone, at Solnhofen in southern Germany. This perfect specimen was later named, in 1861, by Andreas Wagner.

Compsognathus was 74 centimetres (2½ feet) long and weighed as little as 3 kilograms (6½ pounds). It was one of the smallest of the dinosaurs.

There are only two known specimens of *Compsognathus.* The first was found in Germany in the late 1850s, while the second, another excellent specimen, was found in southern France in 1971. At first, the French specimen was thought to be of another species – *C. corallestris* rather than *C. longipes* – because it was larger and the forelimbs seemed to be different. It is now thought that the differences were not so very great and they are now both regarded as being specimens of *C. longipes.*

We know that *Compsognathus* ate lizards, but it also must have caught insects and other small creatures of the undergrowth.

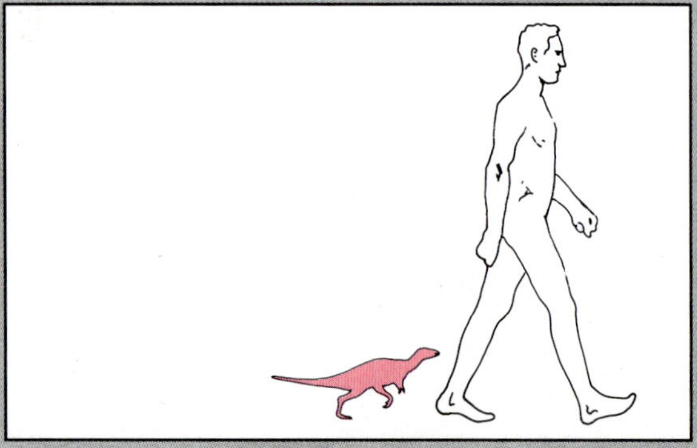

Put feathers on this, the smallest of the dinosaurs, and the result would be almost indistinguishable from the first bird, *Archaeopteryx*. In fact, a fossil unearthed at Solnhofen in 1951 was thought to be a *Compsognathus* until, in 1973, it was proved to be an *Archaeopteryx* specimen. This resemblance is one of the main pieces of evidence to show that the birds are directly descended from the dinosaurs.

Compsognathus and *Archaeopteryx*, along with pterosaurs and all sorts of other reptiles, lived together along the shores of the wooded islands and lagoons of the warm shallow sea that stretched across upper Jurassic Europe. *Compsognathus*, with its chicken-sized body and its nimble little legs, must have been able to run swiftly through the ferny undergrowth and catch fast-moving creatures on the hop. Some bones found in the stomach cavity of the original specimen turned out to be those of a lizard resembling a little iguana.

The French specimen was once mistakenly thought to have flippers on the forelimbs, suggesting that the animal was aquatic.

▶ *Compsognathus* must have been a very swift and agile hunter to be able to run down and catch lizards.

► The hands were very small and carried only two clawed fingers. The feet had three functional toes, plus one small one, and one that was reduced to a sliver of bone.

▼ The skeleton of *Archaeopteryx* is almost identical to that of *Compsognathus* except for the feathers, the longer hands and the bird-like hip.

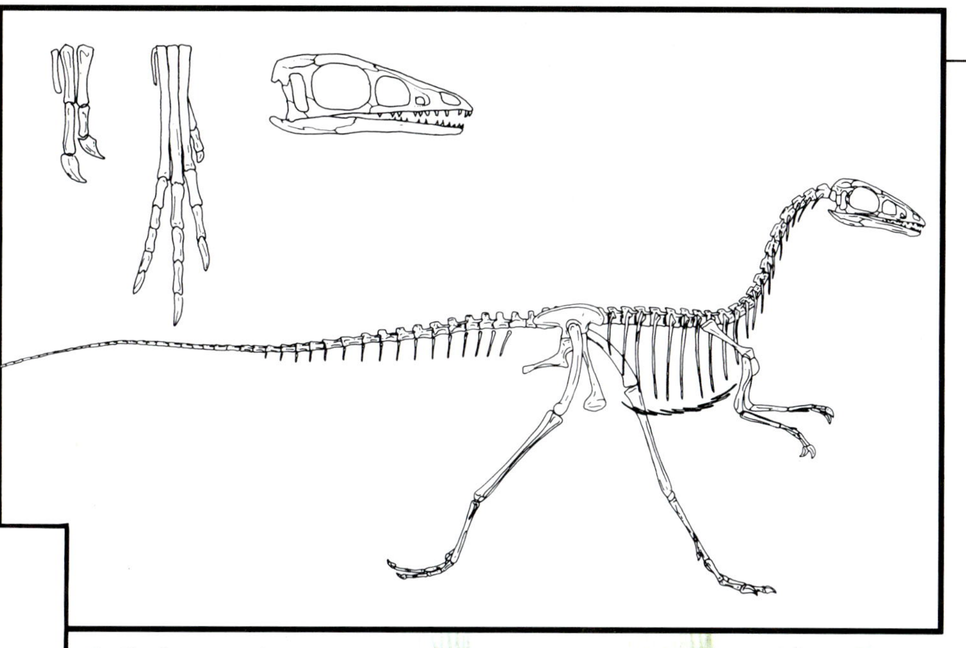

◄ The fine-grained lithographic limestone of southern Germany is formed from limy mud deposited in quiet lagoons. The fossils in it show the minutest detail.

ORNITHOLESTES HERMANI

'HERMAN'S BIRD ROBBER'
THEROPODA, COELUROSAUR
LATE JURASSIC
WYOMING, USA

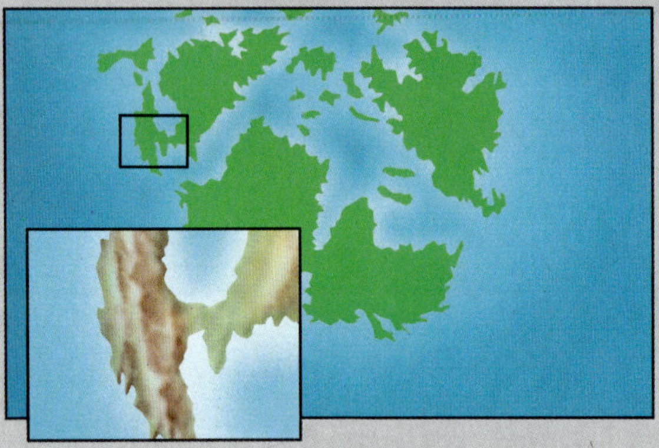

Ornitholestes lived on the lush plains that swept down from the young Rocky Mountains to the shallow sea that covered much of central North America.

In 1900, the partial skeleton of *Ornitholestes* was discovered in the famous dinosaur quarries of Como Bluff in Wyoming. It was first described by Henry Fairfield Osborn in 1903, and re-studied 1916.

In the previous century, in 1879, the backbone of a small dinosaur called *Coelurus* had been unearthed in Bone Cabin Quarry near Como Bluff. There is a distinct possibility that these are specimens of the same animal. Should the two turn out to be the same, then the correct name for *Ornitholestes* would be *Coelurus*, the first name given.

Ornitholestes was about 2 metres (6½ feet) long.

It obviously ate meat of some sort, either caught on the run or scavenged from the carcasses of dead animals.

Ornitholestes looked rather like a small version of one of the big meat-eaters, with its two-footed stance and its short, deep head. Its teeth were stronger and the jaws more powerful than those of other coelurosaurs. It lived in the plains and river deltas of central North America, the landscape that would eventually produce the bone-rich Morrison Formation of rocks. These rocks yield the spectacular skeletons of such giants as *Diplodocus*, *Stegosaurus*, and the larger relatives of *Ornitholestes* such as *Allosaurus* and *Ceratosaurus*.

The name 'bird robber' stems from the idea that *Ornitholestes* may have been agile enough to leap up and catch birds from out of the sky. Its curious hand, with its two fingers and a 'thumb', seems to be suited to this task. However, there are suggestions that it fed on meat from carcasses already killed by the big meat-eaters. It may have darted in between the feet of the meat-eater, grabbed a mouthful of meat, and sprinted out again without disturbing the feast of the larger creatures.

It probably ran about on its hind legs, with its back horizontal, its neck in an S-shaped curve and its head fixed at right angles to it, like the head of a bird. The long stiff tail would have balanced it at the hips.

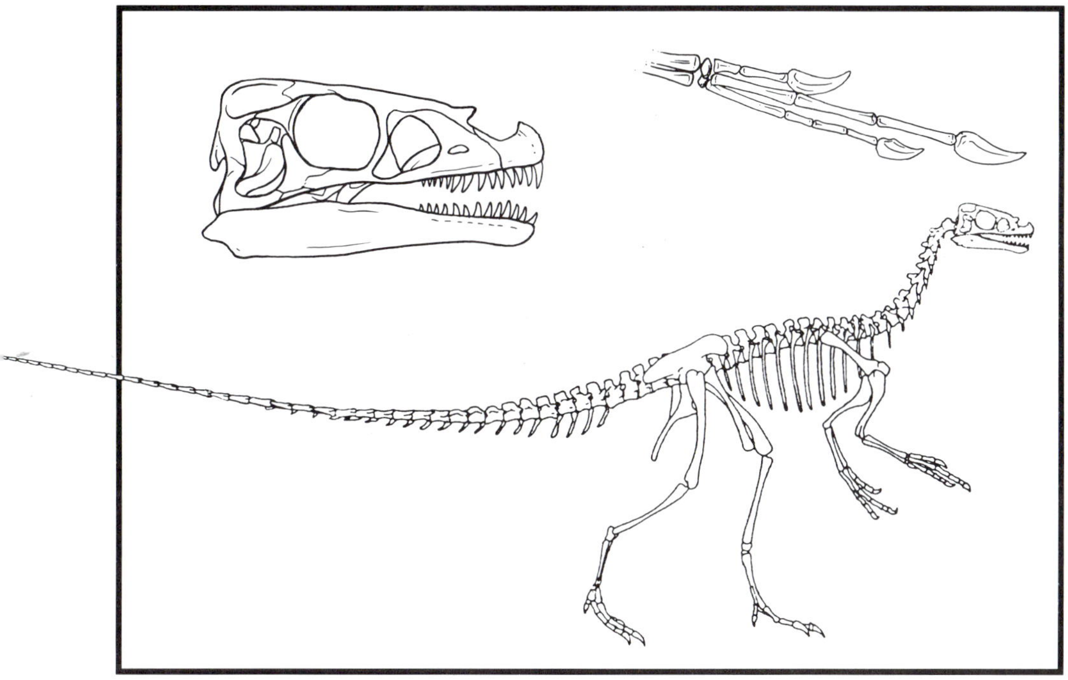

The hand of *Ornitholestes* had two long fingers and a shorter one that could be bent over as a thumb. The palms could be turned to face each other so that the animal could grasp small objects.

The skull was more robust than of any other of the small meat-eaters, and the teeth and jaws were more powerful.

In the forest plains of upper Jurassic North America there was plenty of meat to hunt. *Ornitholestes* may have caught fast-moving animals, or may have eaten from carcasses.

CERATOSAURUS NASICORNIS

'HORNED LIZARD WITH A HORN ON ITS NOSE'

THEROPODA, CARNOSAUR

LATE JURASSIC

NORTH AMERICA AND EAST AFRICA

Ceratosaurus was described in 1884 by the famous pioneer palaeontologist Othniel Charles Marsh. The almost complete skeleton had been discovered the previous year by M.P. Felch. No other skull was found until the 1940s.

The more complete skeletons of *Ceratosaurus* show it to have been about 6.5 metres (22 feet) long, but some isolated bones show that it may have grown much longer.

Ceratosaurus was a meat-eater and probably an active hunter. It may well have hunted in packs, like some of the smaller meat-eaters.

Had we seen this creature prowling through the forested plains and river banks of upper Jurassic North America we would have been quite rightly alarmed. The horn on the nose and the jagged ridge down its back would have made us think that we were looking at a dragon. The curved teeth and the strong claws on the hands would have told us that this monster was a meat-eater. Then we would probably have noticed the rest of its pack stalking along behind it.

Parallel tracks were left on the mud-banks of the rivers, and are now preseved in the sandstones of the famous Morrison Formation of the eastern foothills of the Rocky Mountains in the USA. From these, we can deduce that *Ceratosaurus* was a pack animal, hunting down the big plant-eaters of the time such as *Apatosaurus* and *Diplodocus* (p. 66–7). However, the remains of *Ceratosaurus* are not as common as those of other big meat-eaters, such as *Allosaurus* (p. 60–1). This makes us think that *Ceratosaurus* was a solitary hunter while *Allosaurus* hunted in packs. It is one of the puzzles that palaeontologists still have to solve.

▶ *Ceratosaurus* may have hunted in packs.

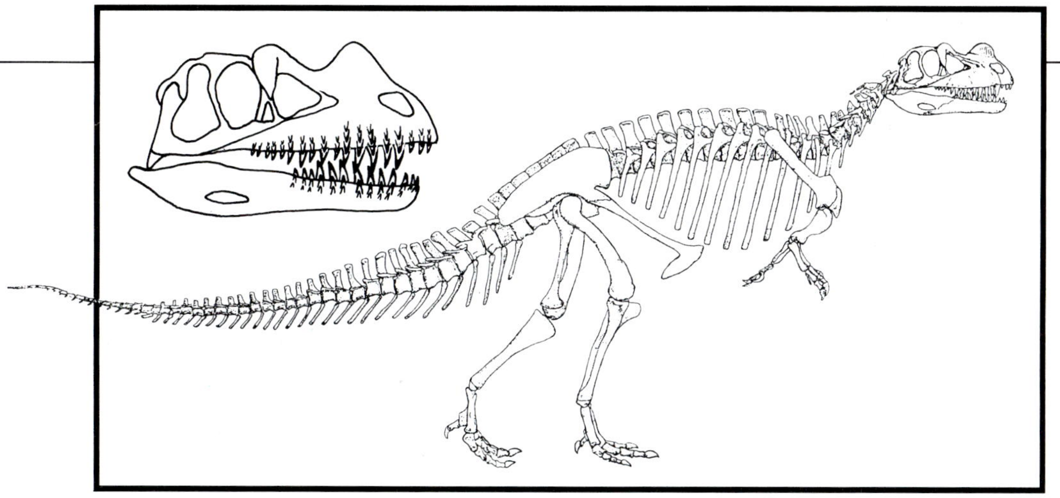

◄ *Ceratosaurus* shed its teeth throughout its life, with new teeth growing to fill in the gaps.

◄ There were four fingers on the hand – most carnosaurs had only three – and the hips were more firmly fused together than is usual in carnosaurs.

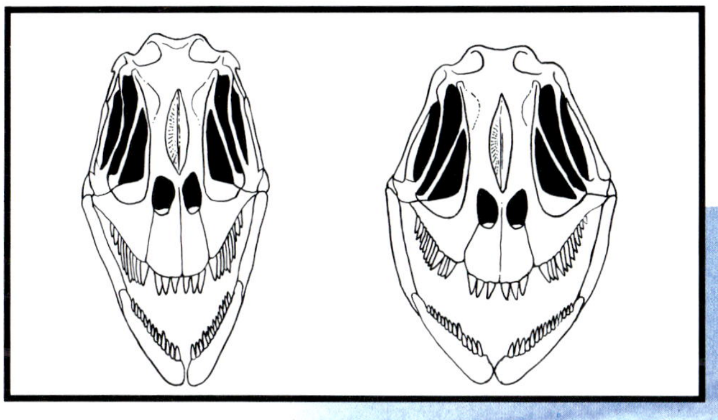

◄ The skull was a loosely-constructed network of bony struts. The whole structure could expand sideways to swallow huge meat chunks.

▼ The head was larger than that of other carnosaurs. As well as the horn above the nose, there were ridges sticking up above the eyes. These might have been used for butting rivals, or for showing off during mating.

ALLOSAURUS FRAGILIS

'DELICATE STRANGE REPTILE'
THEROPODA, CARNOSAUR
LATE JURASSIC
NORTH AMERICA

Allosaurus is one of the best-known of the big meat-eaters, with many individuals having been thoroughly studied. It was first described by Othniel Charles Marsh in 1877 after his assistant, Benjamin Mudge, discovered the remains in the excavations in Colorado, USA. In 1940, a graveyard of over 60 individuals was found in Utah, USA.

In some books, we see *Allosaurus* called *Antrodemus.* This is because a number of bones, found in 1870, had been called *Antrodemus* and it was once thought that these were from the same animal as *Allosaurus.* Now we are not so sure, and *Allosaurus* is the correct name again.

The different specimens of *Allosaurus* are of different sizes, but a typical length is 11 metres (36 feet). The weight has been estimated as 1–2 tonnes.

Allosaurus ate meat, including the largest land animals of the time.

There is a set of tail bones of the giant plant-eater *Apatosaurus* that have been ripped and torn apart with incredible force. The bones are scraped and grooved – and the scrapes and grooves correspond exactly to the spacing of teeth in the jaw of *Allosaurus*. What's more, there are broken *Allosaurus* teeth lying around the scene of the violence, showing the ferocity of the attack. It is quite obvious that *Allosaurus* ate *Apatosaurus*.

How *Allosaurus* was able to eat the huge *Apatosaurus* is still not clear. It could be that *Allosaurus* was simply an extremely powerful hunter, or possibly an entire pack of *Allosaurus* surrounded the *Apatosaurus* and tore it to bits. On the other hand, it may have been that an *Allosaurus* came across the body of the already dead *Apatosaurus* and eaten its fill of it. In an even more dramatic scenario, the *Apatosaurus* may have been savaged to death by an agile pack of *Ceratosaurus* (p. 58–9), and these may have been driven away from their kill by the much larger *Allosaurus* bursting out of the forest upon them.

In any case, the *Allosaurus*, with its tearing talons and its steak-knife teeth, would have made short work of what meat was there.

▶ *Allosaurus* was the largest known of the Jurassic meat-eaters of the Morrison Formation.

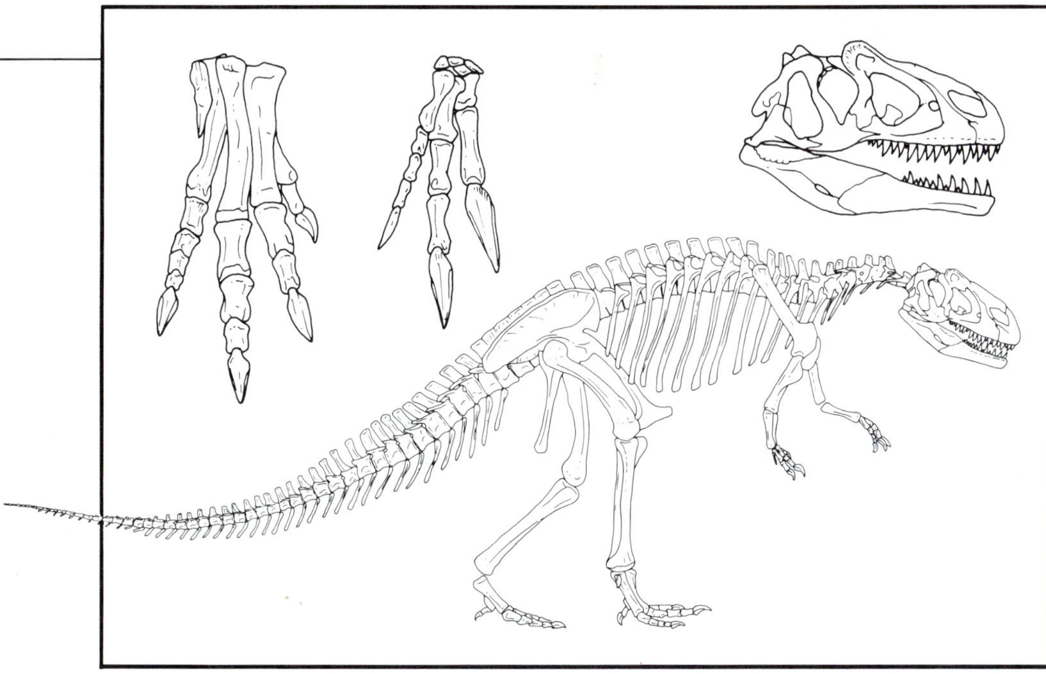

◀ The skull of *Allosaurus* was similar to that of *Ceratosaurus*. Although it had the same flexibility it was more massively built.

◀ The legs were strong, and the feet had three broad weight-bearing toes and a small first toe. The hands had three fingers, two long and one short. All three had enormous talons.

CAMARASAURUS SUPREMUS

'THE BIGGEST CHAMBERED LIZARD'
SAUROPODOMORPHA, SAUROPOD
LATE JURASSIC
NORTH AMERICA

Camarasaurus remains are the most common sauropod remains in the fossil-rich Morrison Formation of late Jurassic North America.

The first sighting of *Camarasaurus* was in 1877 when O.W. Lucas collected some isolated vertebrae in Colorado. Edward Drinker Cope named them. The first description of a complete skeleton was by Charles W. Gilmore in 1925. The skeleton was a young one, and it is very often only a young one that is shown in illustrations.

A fully-grown *Camarasaurus* would have reached a length of 18 metres (60 feet). It was a plant-eater.

The Morrison Formation of late Jurassic rocks stretches north-south along the eastern flanks of the Rocky Mountains between New Mexico and Montana, USA. The water meadows and floodplains that gave rise to this sequence of mudstones and silts must have been the home of all kinds of sauropods. *Diplodocus, Apatosaurus, Brachiosaurus* and many others have been found there. None, however, was more abundant than *Camarasaurus*.

The special characteristic of *Camarasaurus* was its skull. It was big and box-like, full of holes. The teeth were chisel-like and arranged all along the jaws, not bunched at the front as in the diplodocids. The front legs were shorter than the hind, as in most other sauropods, but the shoulders were high so that the back did not slope forward. There were no long upward projections on the vertebrae, so it is unlikely that *Camarasaurus* could have lifted itself up on to its hind legs. The neck and tail were shorter than was usual amongst the sauropods.

The strong teeth show that *Camarasaurus* ate tougher plant material than did the diplodocids. It probably also swallowed stones to help to grind up the food in its stomach. Isolated piles of polished stones found in the Morrison Formation are possibly the results of animals like *Camarasaurus* regurgitating their stomach stones – rather as chickens do when the stones become too worn to grind food.

▶ *Camarasaurus* may have roamed the wooded floodplains of the North American continent in herds.

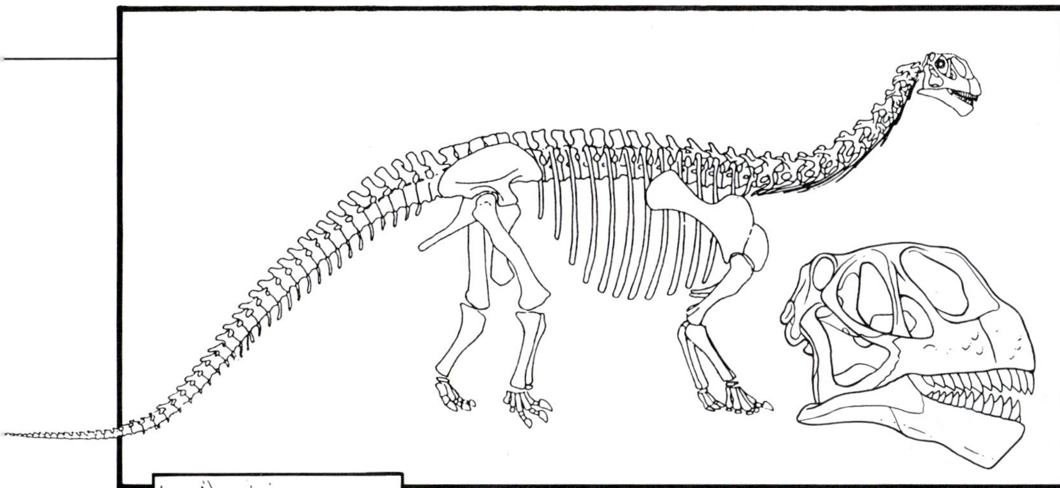

The complete skeleton of *Camarasaurus* shows the animal had a horizontal back between shoulders and hips.

The huge nostrils in front of the eyes probably contained a large area of moist membrane that helped to keep the brain cool in hot weather.

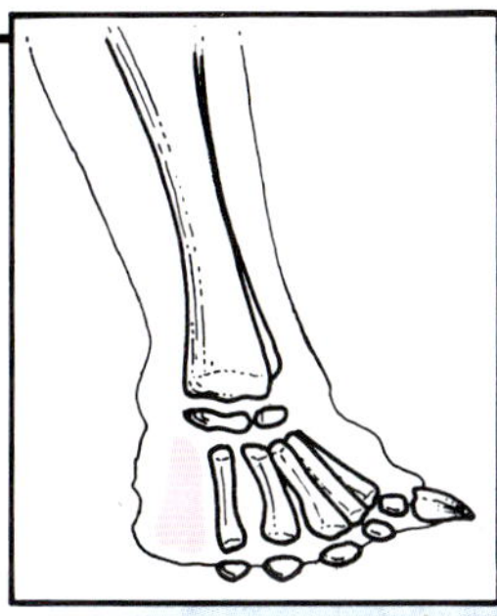

The foot of *Camarasaurus* and the other sauropods probably had a wedge of spongy tissue to take the weight beneath the heel, as modern elephants do.

BRACHIOSAURUS BRANCAI

'BRANCA'S ARM LIZARD'
SAUROPODOMORPHA, SAUROPOD
LATE JURASSIC
NORTH AMERICA AND EAST AFRICA

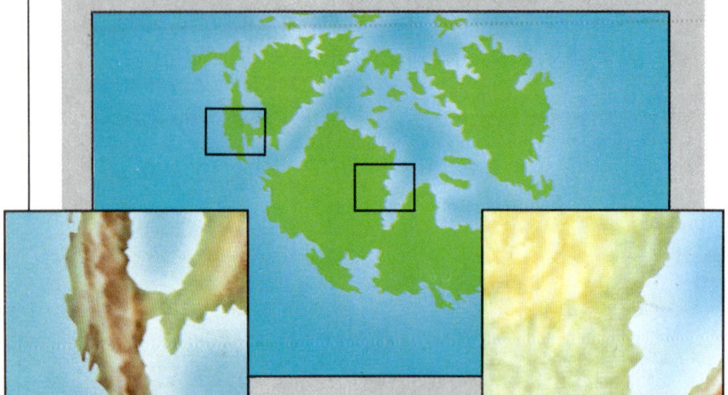

The region of Tanzania in the late Jurassic consisted of wooded river plains, with a winding river cut off from the sea by a series of sandbanks.

Brachiosaurus was first discovered in Colorado, USA, by Elmer Riggs in 1900 and described and named by him in 1903. The most spectacular discovery was by Werner Janensch and Edwin Hennig of the Berlin Museum, in what was then German East Africa (now Tanzania), between 1908 and 1912.

The name 'arm lizard' refers to the particularly long forelimbs. 'Branca' was Dr W. Branca, the director of the Berlin Museum who mounted the East African expedition.

Brachiosaurus was 22.5 metres (74 feet) long and, as the Berlin skeleton is mounted, 12 metres (39 feet high). It must have weighed something like 75 tons.

Brachiosaurus was a plant-eater, probably moving about in herds and browsing from the tops of trees.

The brachiosaurids differed from the other main sauropod group, the diplodocids, in that the front legs were longer than the hind, so that the back sloped up from the hips to the shoulders. The shoulders were then at a height of about 5 metres (16 feet) above the ground and provided a foundation for the almost vertical neck. The structure of the skeleton shows that the animal would not have been able to rear up on its hind legs as the diplodocids were able to do – with a neck like that it would hardly have needed to! The brachiosaurs were the giraffes of the late Jurassic and early Cretaceous woodlands, although they would have been able to reach up to twice the height of any giraffe today.

Big as it was, *Brachiosaurus* would not have been the biggest brachiosaurid. The remains of even larger and heavier creatures have been discovered in Colorado, USA. When the bones were compared to the bones of *Brachiosaurus*, it was realized that they could have belonged to a beast that weighed 130 tonnes! Unfortunately, they are only odd pieces of fossil bone, and it is unlikely that we will ever have a clear idea of what the whole animal looked like.

▲ Some scientists think the huge nostrils on top of the *Brachiosaurus* skull meant that it had a trunk, like today's elephants.

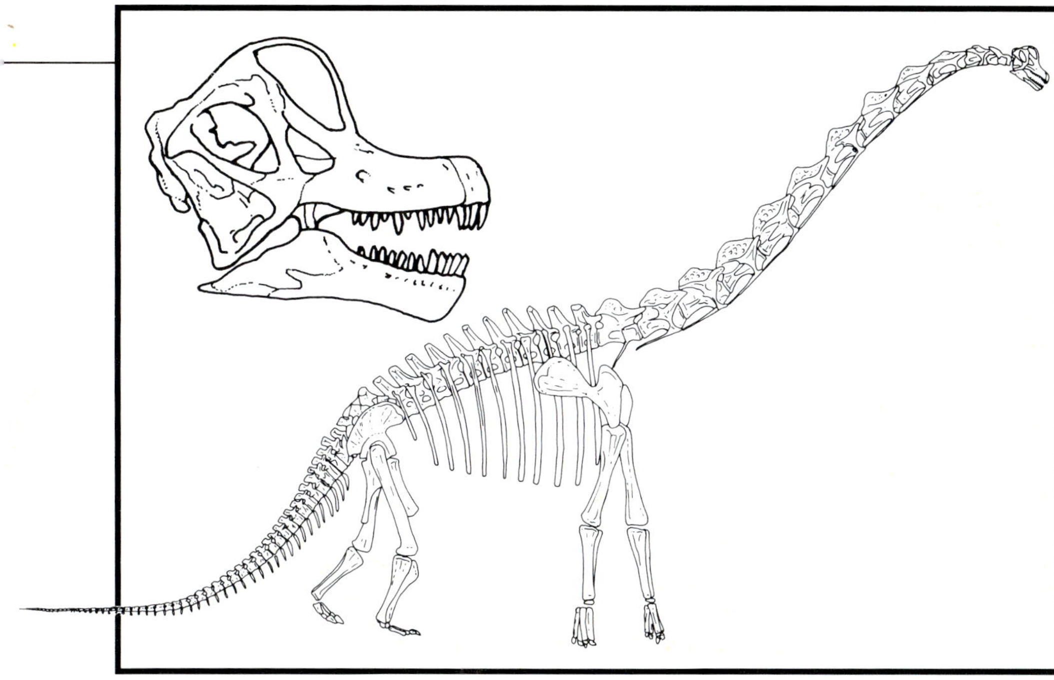

▲ The skull had the nostrils at the very top. The teeth were large and chisel-shaped.

▼ *Brachiosaurus* probably roamed the wooded plains in herds, browsing from the tops of trees.

▲ The complete skeleton shows the incredible height of the neck and the very long forelimbs.

DIPLODOCUS LONGUS

'LONG DOUBLE BEAMED ANIMAL'
SAUROPODOMORPHA, SAUROPOD
LATE JURASSIC AND EARLY CRETACEOUS
NORTH AMERICA AND SOUTHERN ENGLAND

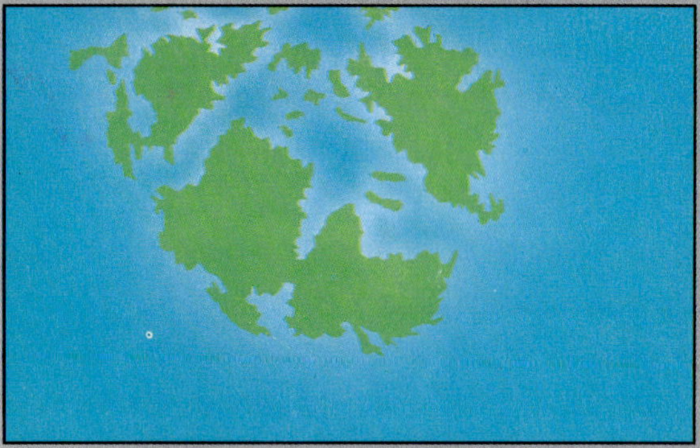

The first *Diplodocus* remains consisted of tail and hind limb bones, discovered by Samuel Williston near Canyon City, Colorado, USA, in 1877. They were given the name *Diplodocus longus* by Othniel Charles Marsh. Better skeletons were found in Wyoming in 1899 and a particularly fine skeleton was recovered from Utah in 1902. This was named *D. carnegii,* after Andrew Carnegie, the steel millionaire whose money financed the excavation of the fossil. Ten casts of the skeleton were sent to various museums throughout the world. In Britain, *Diplodocus* bones were found on the Isle of Wight, southern England,. in 1977 and footprints identified as those of *Diplodocus* were discovered in Dorset in 1987.

The 'double beam', referred to in the name, is a reference to the paired skids below the tail vertebra. These protected the tail if it dragged along the ground.

Diplodocus was 27 metres (87 feet) long. But it was quite a lightweight dinosaur, weighing only about 10 tons.

Diplodocus was a plant-eater, and browsed conifer needles and cones from the tops of trees.

Imagine you are climbing a tree. You are about 10 metres (about 35 feet) above the ground when, suddenly, a gentle-looking head, no bigger than that of a horse, pushes its way through the branches and strips the leaves off the twigs close to you. You would hardly imagine that head belonged to an animal that was longer than three buses. It would have been able to rear up to such heights using the powerful muscles of the back – something few people realized until recently.

The overall impression given by a *Diplodocus* would have been one of length. Most of its length was neck and tail. The tail ended in a whiplash that was probably used for defence.

Despite all this, there were longer animals than *Diplodocus*. A close relative of *Diplodocus* was discovered in the rocks of New Mexico in 1984. It has not yet been fully excavated, but it seems to have been about 33 metres (110 feet) long – the longest living thing yet discovered. It has been given the provisional name 'seis-mosaurus' – the earth-shaker.

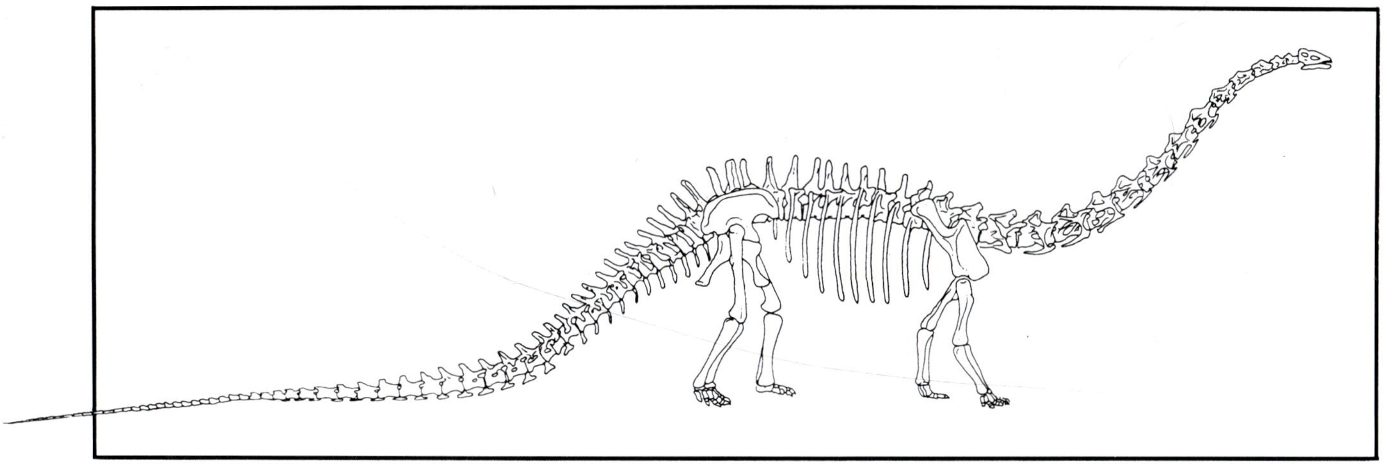

▲ Many skeletons of *Diplodocus* have been found.

▼ The back muscles would have allowed *Diplodocus* to raise its forelimbs off the ground enabling it to reach high into the trees.

▲ There were five toes on all four feet. Three toes on the rear feet had claws, while the forefeet had one clawed toe. The tall spines from the vertebrae at the hips, the lower part of the back and the base of the tail were anchor points for strong back muscles.

▼ The teeth were pencil-like and confined to the front of the jaw. The nostrils were on the top of the head.

MAMENCHISAURUS HOCHUANENSIS

'LIZARD FROM HOCHUAN AND MAMENCHI'
SAUROPODOMORPHA, SAUROPOD
LATE JURASSIC
CHINA

Bones of this odd diplodocid first came to light in Sichuan Province of South-Central China in 1952 and they were given the name *Mamenchisaurus constructus* by Young Chung Chein. More remains were found in 1957, but it was not until 1972 that an almost complete skeleton was described.

The Mamenchi and Hochuan, referred to in the name, are place names in south-central China.

The most complete skeleton of *Mamenchisaurus* measures 18.5 metres (62 feet), but much of the tail is missing. The entire animal was probably about 23 metres (80 feet) long. The neck itself measures 8.9 metres (33 feet).

Like other sauropods, it was a plant-eater.

Kunglung – terrible dragon – is the Chinese name for dinosaur. Since the 1950s there have been many dinosaur discoveries in China, and *Mamenchisaurus* is probably the most spectacular.

The incredibly long neck was made up of 19 vertebrae. Each vertebra was scooped out, leaving nothing but an immensely strong hollow framework. This is a feature of most of the big sauropods. In this way, the weight of the bone could be cut down but the strength kept. Each neck vertebra was strapped to the next by strips of bone and the result was a very stiff and rigid structure. The only bending could have been done at the head end or the shoulder end.

What could such a neck have been used for? If we can imagine *Mamenchisaurus* rising up on its hind legs as the other diplodocids seem to have been able to do, then the animal could have reached leaves and twigs at heights of over 15 metres (50 feet)! Another idea is that the sauropods may have spent much of their time in ponds and lakes. If that were the case, then *Mamenchisaurus* could have swept its neck about, scooping up water weed from great areas of the water surface.

The neck is so unusual that many palaeontologists do not regard *Mamenchisaurus* as a diplodocid, but put it in a group of its own.

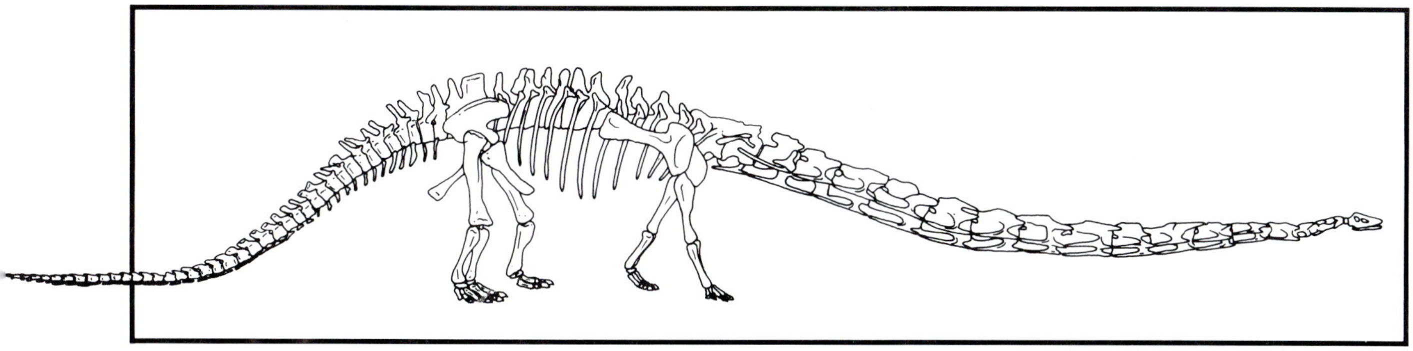

The bones of the neck are well represented in the most complete skeleton, although parts of the body and tail are missing.

The great neck, with its 19 vertebrae, must have allowed the animal to reach food over a vast area.

The long neck may have allowed *Mamenchisaurus* to reach up to the topmost branches of the trees or, alternatively, to sweep water plants from the surface of ponds and lakes.

Mamenchisaurus had the longest neck of any known animal.

STEGOSAURUS ARMATUS

'ARMOURED ROOF LIZARD'
STEGOSAURIA, STEGOSAURID
LATE JURASSIC
NORTH AMERICA – PARTICULARLY COLORADO, WHERE IT IS THE STATE FOSSIL

Many stegosaur remains were excavated from quarries in Colorado and Wyoming in the 1870s and 1880s by teams sent by Othniel Charles Marsh. Marsh published the first account of these remains in 1877. He did not publish a description of the full skeleton until 1891.

Stegosaurus was the largest of the known stegosaurs, reaching a length of 7.4 metres (25 feet) and a weight of 3500 kilograms (4 tons).

It ate plants, probably grazing close to the ground and also browsing from the low branches of trees.

Stegosaurus must be one of the most familiar of the dinosaurs, with its splendid array of plates on its back, its spiky tail and its tiny head. For all that, there is still a great deal of discussion and argument amongst palaeontologists about just how the plates were arranged and for what they were used.

There were two rows of plates – no one disputes that. However, were they arranged in pairs, or were they staggered? *Stegosaurus* tends to be fossilized with the plates overlapping one another, but this is probably due to their movement as the carcass rotted. Other stegosaurs have smaller plates and spines and these appear to be definitely arranged in pairs. If that is so, then why should *Stegosaurus's* plates not also be so arranged?

Now, what was the function of the plates? The traditional explanation is that they formed a kind of armour, protecting the backbone. However, work done in the 1970s suggests that they were more likely to be heat-regulating devices, like the sail of *Spinosaurus* (p. 96–7). If that is so, then it would make more sense if the plates were arranged in a staggered pattern.

▲ Different stegosaurs had different plate arrangements. The one with four pairs of tail spikes is *Stegosaurus ungulatus.* The one with very large plates on its back is probably a related stegosaur, *Diracodon.*

▶ If the plates were used as heat regulators, then *Stegosaurus's* only defence would have been the two pairs of spikes on the tail.

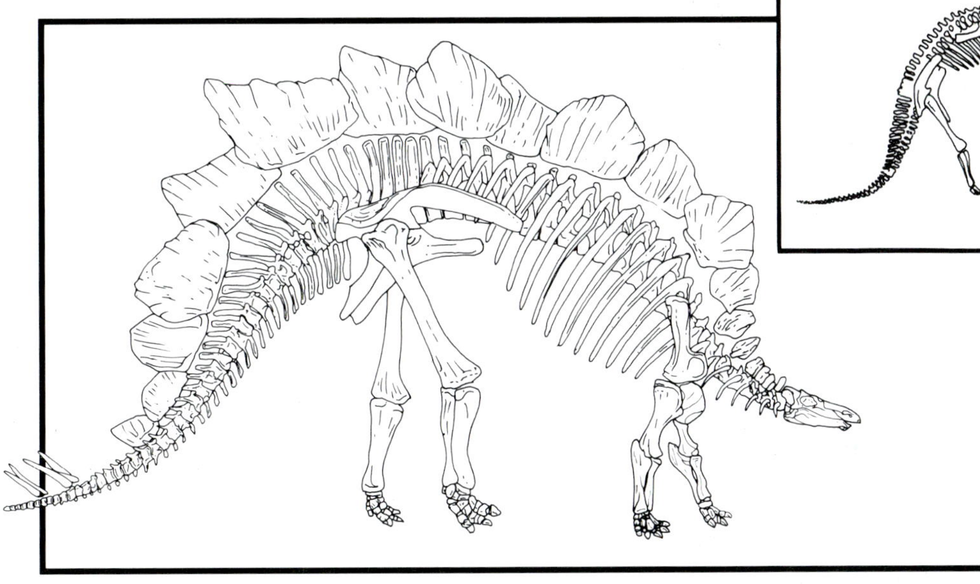

▲ The long spines on the backbone above the hips would suggest the presence of strong muscles here. The leverage produced by these muscles could easily have allowed *Stegosaurus* to rear up on its hind legs and reach the twigs and leaves of low branches.

KENTROSAURUS AETHIOPICUS

'POINTED LIZARD FROM AFRICA'
STEGOSAURIA, STEGOSAURID
LATE JURASSIC
TANZANIA

This was one of the important dinosaur discoveries made by the German expedition to East Africa in 1909–1912. It was described and named by Edwin Hennig, one of the three palaeontologists on the expedition, in 1915. There is a mounted skeleton in the Palaeontological Museum of Humboldt University, East Berlin, but most of the other *Kentrosaurus* bones were lost when the museum was damaged by Allied bombing during World War II.

Kentrosaurus was a small stegosaur, only reaching a length of 2.5 metres (8 feet).

It was a plant-eater.

The upper Jurassic animals of Tendaguru, in Tanzania, were very similar to those that existed in North America at the same time, found in the Morrison Formation on the eastern flank of the Rocky Mountains. This indicates that these two places had the same geographical and climatic conditions, and that they were both part of one continent.

Kentrosaurus was the African version of *Stegosaurus*. It was a much smaller and slimmer animal and its plates and spines were rather different. Over its neck, shoulders and the forward half of its back there were narrow plates. Then the spikes began, and these stuck out in majestic pairs down the rest of the back to the tip of the tail. Another pair stuck out sideways from the hips. There does not seem to be much doubt that these were used for defence, and not for heat control as may have been the case with *Stegosaurus*. Also, unlike *Stegosaurus*, the backbone did not have pronounced spines in the hip and tail region, so *Kentrosaurus* would not have been able to rear up on its hind legs.

▼ The plates of *Kentrosaurus* were quite narrow, and the spikes were really spectacular.

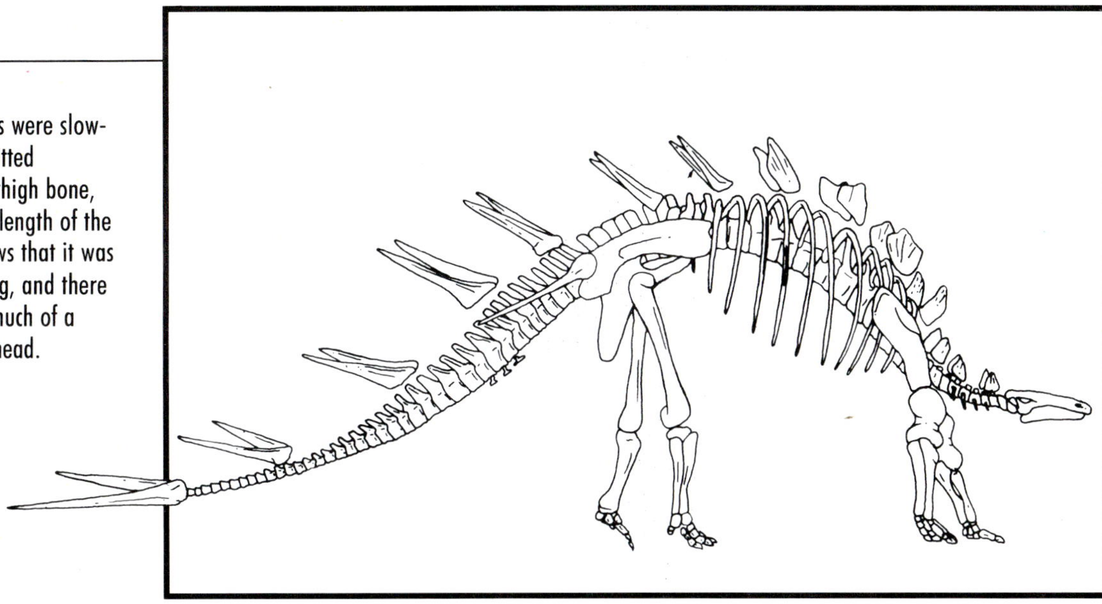

The stegosaurs were slow-moving and dull-witted animals. The long thigh bone, compared with the length of the rest of the leg, shows that it was not built for running, and there was not room for much of a brain in the small head.

Other stegosaurs had spines about the hips as well. *Lexovisoaurus* from England and France may have looked very much like *Kentrosaurus*.

EARLY CRETACEOUS GEOGRAPHY

In the early part of the Cretaceous, from about 144 million years ago onwards, Gondwana – the southern half of Pangaea – was beginning to scatter. Antarctica, New Zealand and Australia broke away as a single lump. So did India and Madagascar. In the west, South America was beginning to break away from Africa. Rift valleys had formed along the complete boundary between the two, and inlets of the ocean, like the modern Red Sea, reached northwards from the south and eastwards from the area of the Caribbean. By the end of the early Cretaceous, these two had met and the two continents had separated. The southern end of this area had been stretching, and throwing up volcanoes, since Triassic times.

Seaways still existed between North America and Europe, but the continents had not yet begun to break apart. Europe was still a mass of islands, but the islands were much larger – one island alone covered the entire land area of today's British Isles. The shallow seas caught between them tended to dry out into freshwater lakes as the sea levels lowered and the islands grew. One such lake – The Wealden Lake – stretched from southern England across to northern Germany. Further east, beyond the Ural Archipelago, the Ob Basin still covered much of northern Asia, but it was now smaller.

Australia seemed to open up and sink. Shallow seas flooded in from the north and covered most of the interior.

The Sundance Sea still lay across much of North America, and the Rocky Mountains were beginning to reach their present height. Over on the other side of Laurasia – still the most complete section of the old Pangaea – island arcs and chains of volcanoes were forming along the edge of Panthalassa. This edge was looking like today's Pacific coast of Asia, with island arcs, shallow seas and deep trenches. As Pangaea split up and spread outwards, the ocean beds were being swallowed up.

▶ The supercontinent was in tatters. Seaways split Gondwana into pieces and separated these from Laurasia. This made the migration of animal life increasingly difficult. Animals developing in one area could now be quite different from those developing in another, evolving in isolation. Only when a lowering of the sea level produced land bridges, or when an isthmus (a narrow piece of land connecting two larger bodies) was produced from a chain of volcanic islands, could animals spread from one continent to another.

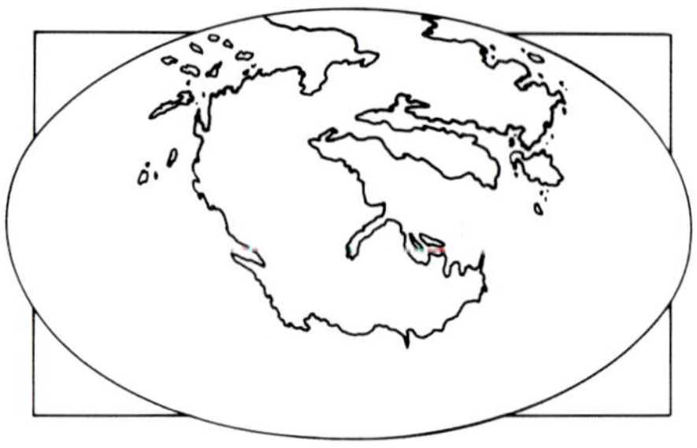

TRIASSIC
215 million years ago

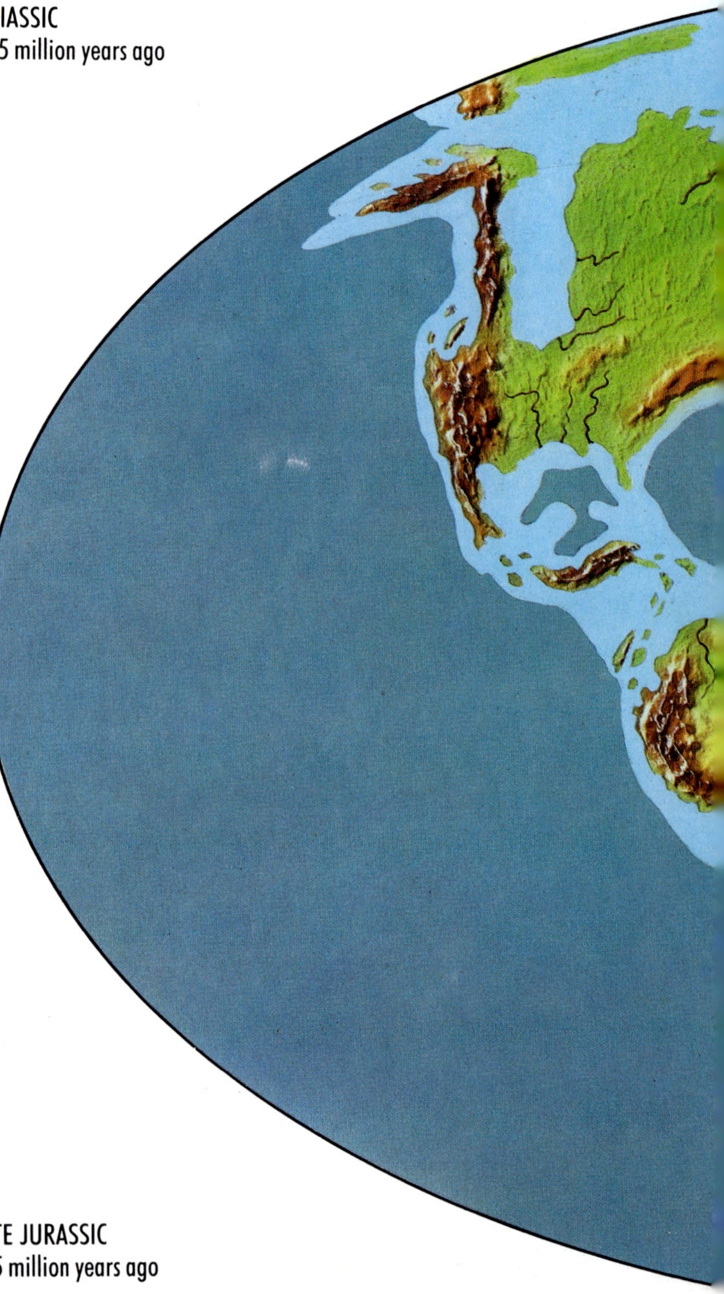

LATE JURASSIC
145 million years ago

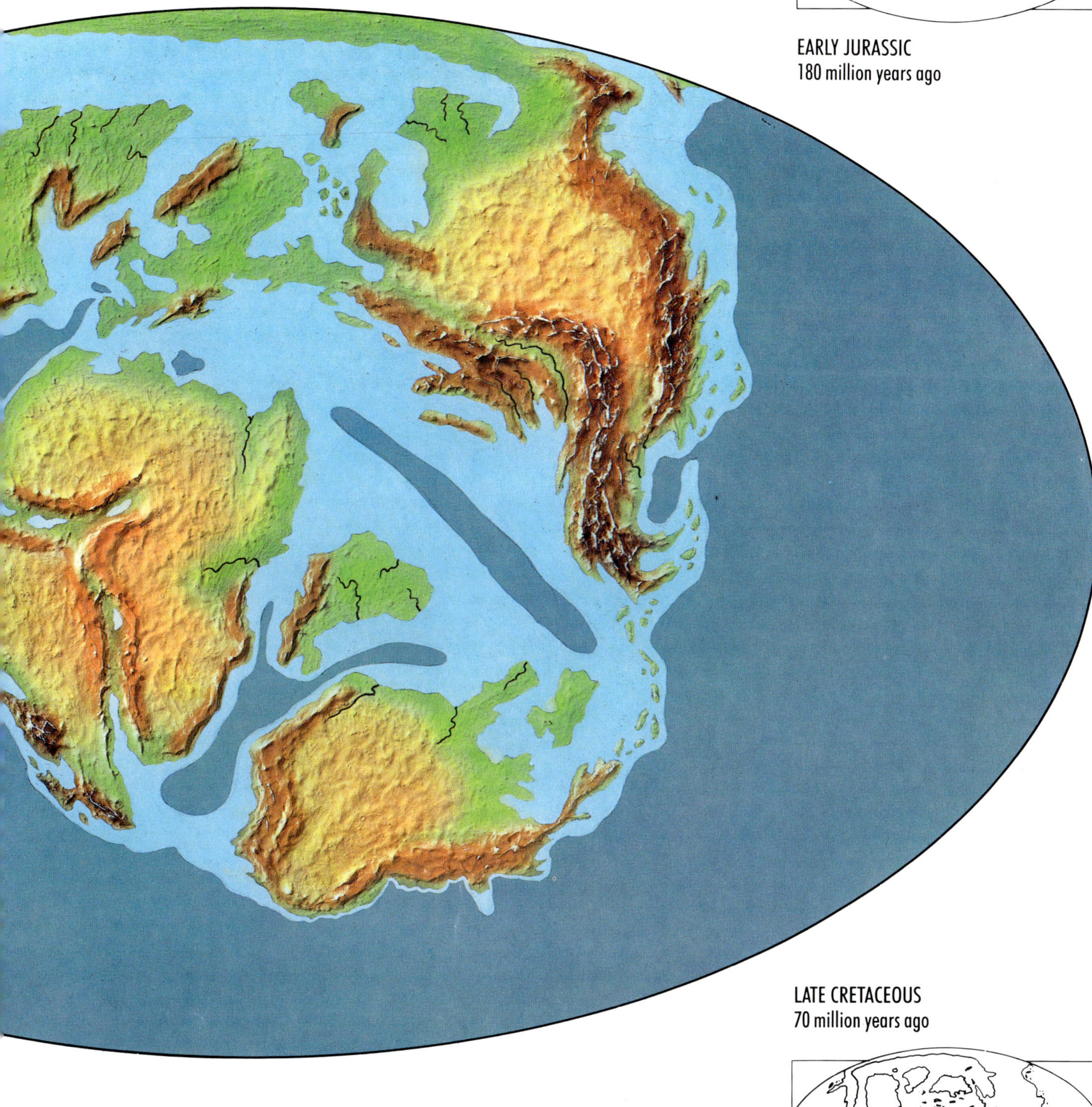

EARLY JURASSIC
180 million years ago

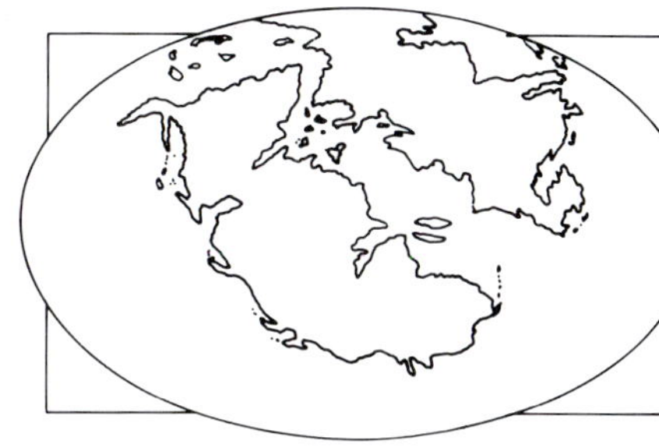

LATE CRETACEOUS
70 million years ago

EARLY CRETACEOUS CONDITIONS

The climate of the early Cretaceous continued to be warm and mild, as in the Jurassic. Even at the poles, the weather was not extreme. Nowadays, we have ice caps at both the North and South Poles. This is a freak of geography. The continent of Antarctica now lies over the South Pole and so the Pole is far from the warming influence of the sea. Thus, it is very cold there. The North Pole is in a sea area, but this sea area is almost land-locked. There is no circulation of water between it and the warmer oceans of the Earth, and so it is very cold there also. In Mesozoic times the North and the South Poles lay in sea areas, and these seas were connected to the seas in the warmer parts of the world. The circulation of currents meant that cold water was always carried away from the poles and warm water was always brought towards them. Therefore, although the weather might have been cold, there were no permanent ice caps.

On land, the forests of Jurassic-type plants – conifers, ginkgoes, cycads, and undergrowths of ferns and horsetails – still flourished. On the shores of the Wealden Lake in southern England and Belgium the horsetail beds were grazed by herds of *Iguanadon* (p. 86–7) and *Hypsilophodon* (p. 84–5), stalked by the ever-hungry

▼ Most of the early Cretaceous dinosaurs that are known to us lived in the woodlands by the broad Wealden Lake in northern Europe. As well as the dinosaurs, crocodiles lived in the small rivers and streams winding across the plains, and pterosaurs like *Ornithodesmus* lived amongst the trees.

Megalosaurus (p. 78–9), while *Baryonyx* (p. 80–1) fished the many rivers of the lowland plains.

In some places the climate was drier than it had been. In North America the rising Rocky Mountains threw up a barrier between the great ocean and the main part of the continent. Through the scrubby vegetation of this area hunted the fierce packs of *Deinonychus* (p. 82–3). In the dry areas of northern Africa, a long way from the moist winds of the sea, the sail-backed *Ouranosaurus* (p. 88–9) foraged for food amongst the desert bushes. The arid interior of eastern Asia also had dinosaurs, such as the small, parrot-like *Psittacosaurus* (p. 90–1).

Sea life was still abundant. The ichthyosaurs were dying out now, their place taken by the mosasaurs – animals related to the lizards but with huge crocodile-shaped bodies and paddles for limbs. The largest of the short-necked pliosaurs, *Kronosaurus*, lived in the shallow interior seas of Australia at this time.

▶ Although the world's geography now consisted of continents, rather than supercontinents, some areas were still very far from the sea. As always, these areas tended to be very much drier than places closer to the coasts. Central North America was one such place, but dinosaurs still existed there.

▶ Early Cretaceous shallow seas were still full of life. The ammonites continued to be abundant. Big sea reptiles still existed, including the biggest and heaviest of the short-necked pliosaurs – *Kronosaurus* of Australia – which must have been a kind of reptilian version of a sperm whale.

MEGALOSAURUS BUCKLANDI

'BUCKLAND'S BIG LIZARD'
THEROPODA, MEGALOSAURID
JURASSIC AND EARLY CRETACEOUS
EUROPE AND AFRICA

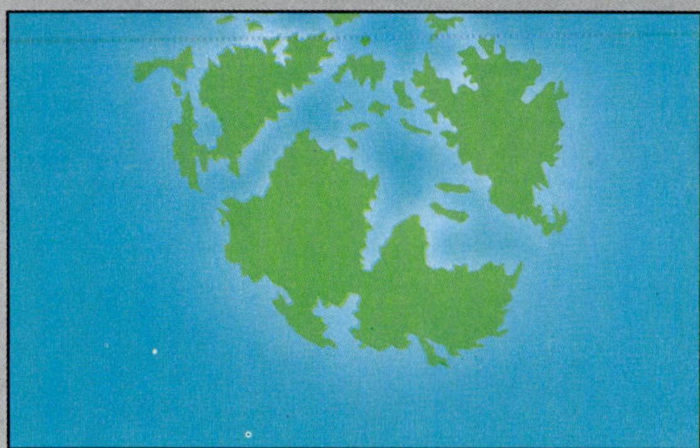

Megalosaurus was the first dinosaur to be recognized. Its name first appeared in an article written in 1822 by the physician James Parkinson. This described a jawbone and teeth being studied by William Buckland, the famous pioneer palaeontologist. In 1824, Buckland himself wrote a fuller scientific account of the fossil.

Over the last 150 years a great many fossil bones have been called *Megalosaurus*, but there are no complete skeletons in existence. At times, it was customary to name all theropod remains from Europe '*Megalosaurus*'. Now many of the best '*Megalosaurus*' remains have been given other names.

A *Megalosaurus* would have been about 9 metres (30 feet) long and would have weighed about a tonne.

It was a meat-eater.

The place of *Megalosaurus* in the history of palaeontology – as the first dinosaur to be described – makes it an important animal. Yet, we still don't have a very clear idea of what it looked like. At first, with nothing to compare it with, the early palaeontologists restored it as a dragon-like animal with a huge head and walking on all fours. It was not until similar theropods began to be discovered in North America several decades later, that people realized it must have been a two-legged animal.

The head was large and had sharp meat-tearing teeth. The neck was very flexible. The body was balanced at the hips by a long tail behind. The legs were massive, to support its weight, and there were probably three main toes and a smaller one turned back. The arms were smaller than the legs and may have had three, or four, fingers.

▶ The first fossil ever to be identified as a dinosaur fossil was this jawbone and teeth of *Megalosaurus*, found in Oxford, England.

▶ This famous, and often-reproduced, drawing of *Megalosaurus* by Friedrich von Huene of the University of Tübingeng, W. Germany, used the backbones of one of the spinosaurs, *Altispinax* (p. 96–7), hence the deep ridge down its back.

▼ *Megalosaurus* was a hunter of *Iguanodon* in the lowland forests and glades of Jurassic and Lower Cretaceous northern Europe.

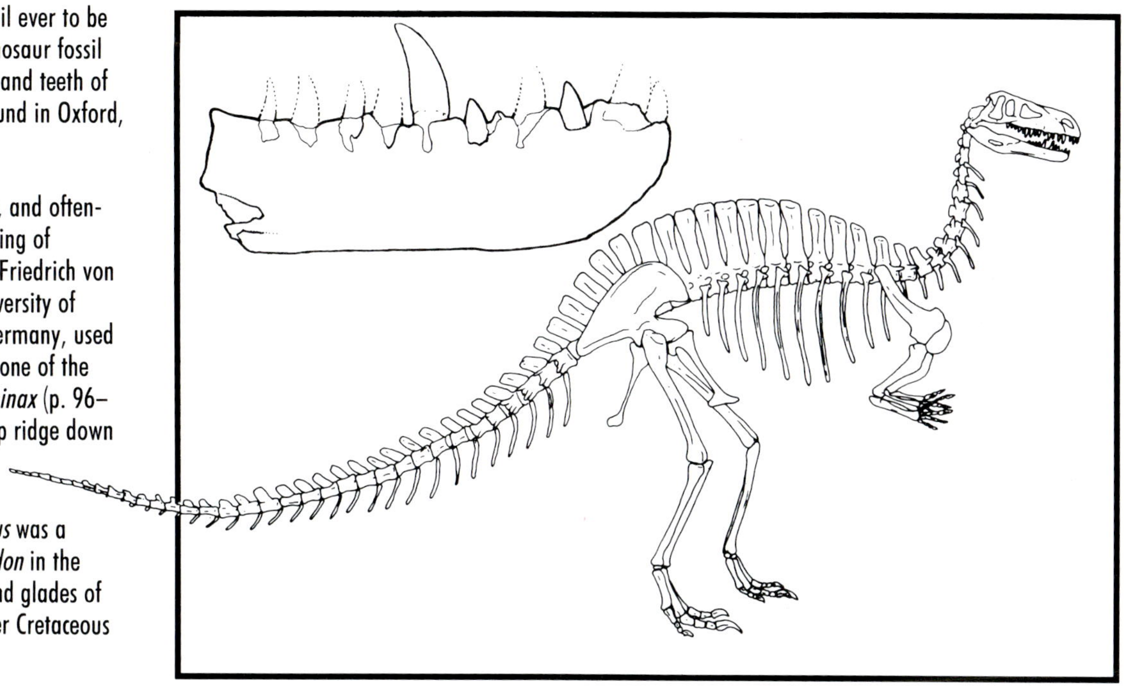

BARYONYX WALKERI

'WALKER'S HEAVY CLAW'
THEROPODA, BARYONYCHID
EARLY CRETACEOUS
SOUTHERN ENGLAND

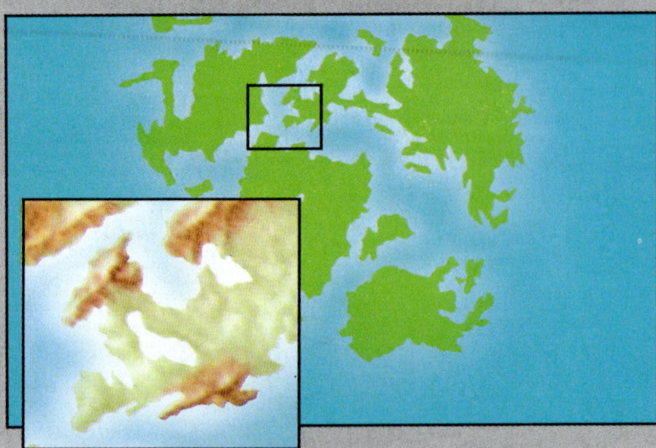

Deltas and river plains spread from uplands in the area of London, England, toward the Wealden Lake that covered much of northern Europe.

Baryonyx was first described in 1986 by Dr Alan Charig and Dr Angela Milner of the British Museum (Natural History) in London. The skeleton was found, in 1983, by amateur fossil collector William Walker, after whom it is named. The only skeleton so far found is a good one, with about 70 per cent of the bones present.

The first part of the skeleton to be found was the enormous claw that Walker saw sticking out of the side of a clay-pit.

Baryonyx was about 6 metres (20 feet) long.

It was probably a fish-eater.

Baryonyx may have fished the rivers that flowed into the great Wealden Lake, which stretched across northern Europe in Lower Cretaceous times.

Baryonyx breaks all the rules for flesh-eating dinosaurs! It probably moved about on its hind legs, but its forelegs were very large for this kind of animal, and so it may have spent much of its time on all fours. Like some other flesh-eaters it possessed an enormous killing claw. However, unlike the others, this claw was on the hand rather than on the foot. (At least scientists think that that is the case, since the bones of the arms were so powerful.) The neck was quite long but it was not very flexible and the head was not perched at right angles to it, as it is in other theropods. The jaws were particularly long and crocodile-like, with twice as many teeth as other meat-eaters. There was a crest on the snout.

The large number of teeth, the long jaws and the presence of fish-scales in the body cavity seem to suggest that *Baryonyx* ate fish. In that case, the function of the claw would be obvious. The great creature would probably have crouched on a river bank, or even in the river itself, and hooked out the fish as they swam by – just like grizzly bears do today.

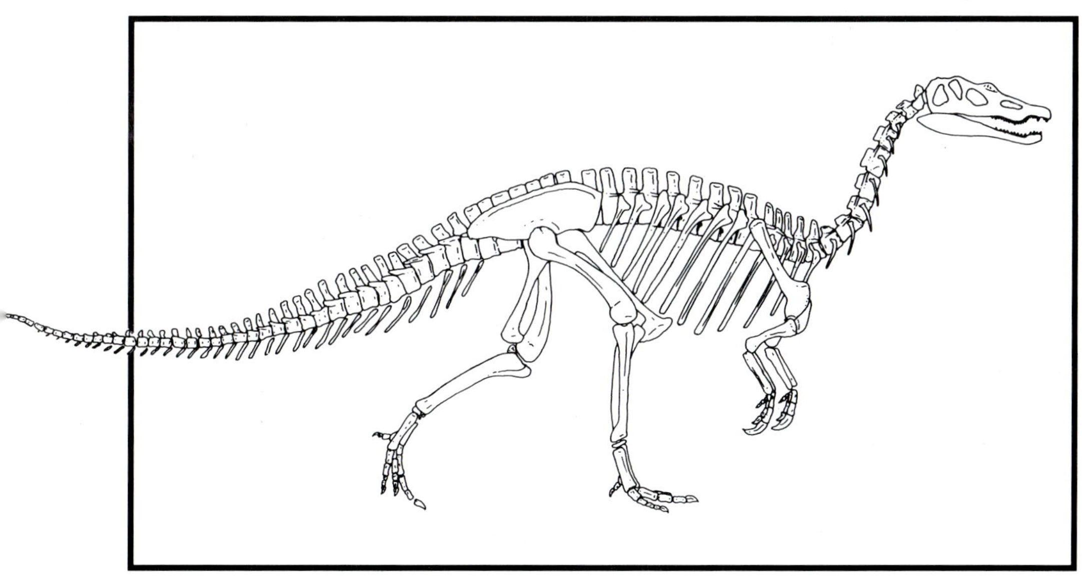

▲ The four-footed stance and the lack of an S-shaped curve to the neck would have given the impression of a very long, low animal.

◀ The skull had crocodile-like jaws with many teeth and a crest.

◀ There were *Iguanodon* bones found with the *Baryonyx* skeleton. It may have eaten any dead thing it found.

DEINONYCHUS ANTIRRHOPUS

'TERRIBLE CLAW AND OPPOSING HANDS'
THEROPODA, DROMAEOSAURID
EARLY CRETACEOUS
WESTERN NORTH AMERICA

Deinonychus was uncovered in 1964 from a hillside in Montana, USA, and the definitive account of it was published in 1969 by John Ostrom, its discoverer.

A fully grown *Deinonychus* was 3–4 metres (10–12 feet) long and stood, perhaps, 1.5 metres (5 feet) high. As usual, most of the length was tail, and the whole animal would have weighed only about 70–77 kilograms (150–170 pounds).

Deinonychus probably hunted in packs like modern wolves, and could bring down prey animals much larger than themselves.

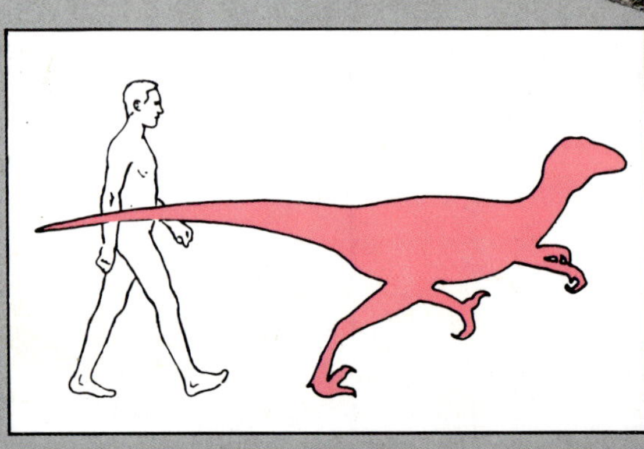

We used to imagine that the most ferocious and terrible of meat-eating dinosaurs were the huge carnivores, like *Tyrannosaurus* (p.98–9) and *Ceratosaurus* (p.58–9), that stalked like ogres over the warm continents of the Jurassic and Cretaceous periods. That was until the discovery of the lightweight *Deinonychus* in 1964. The find was so remarkable that its discoverer, John Ostrom, referred to it as 'An Unusual Theropod' in the title of his scientific report.

It must have been a very active hunter, as we can see by the build of the limbs. The whole animal was nicely balanced at the hips by a long, stiff, rod-like tail. Each foot consisted of two toes that carried the creature's weight, and a third that was modified into the most wicked-looking talon. This talon was obviously the hunter's main weapon. It appears that *Deinonychus* could stand on one foot and slash with the claw on the other, using the tail as a balancing pole. The brain was big enough to handle the complicated coordination for this. The killing claw could be retracted and lifted out of the way when the animal was walking or running. The hands were also very large. Each had three long clawed fingers, useful for holding on to the struggling prey while the flick-knife hind claw did its work.

▼ The very bird-like build has made some palaeontologists think that *Deinonychus* may have been covered with feathers. The insulation would help keep the animal's temperature constant – something necessary for its active lifestyle.

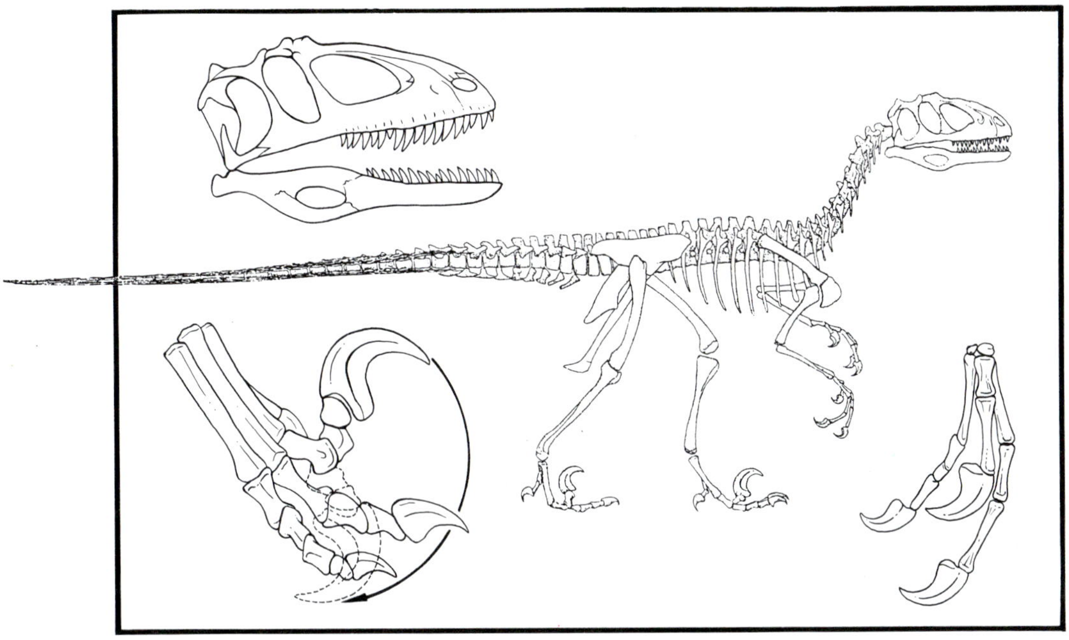

The skeleton was bird-like, especially in the way that the skull made an angle with the neck. The exact shape of the hips is not known. They could have been lizard-like or bird-like.

The bones of the hand were like those of the earliest birds, suggesting that *Deinonychus's* ancestors were close to those of the birds.

Deinonychus must have been as large and as fierce as a modern leopard. It was the 'sabre-toothed tiger' of the Lower Cretaceous forests, hunting in packs for animals larger than itself.

HYPSILOPHODON FOXI

'FOX'S HIGH RIDGED TOOTH'
ORNITHOPODA, HYPSILOPHODONTID
EARLY CRETACEOUS
SOUTHERN ENGLAND, PORTUGAL AND SOUTH DAKOTA, USA

The first bones of *Hypsilophodon* were uncovered in England in 1849, but they were thought to have belonged to a baby *Iguanodon* (p. 86–7). The first proper description was made in 1870 by T.H. Huxley. Since then many skeletons have been discovered, especially on the Isle of Wight, southern England.

The 1870 description was made from several skeletons discovered in 1868 by the Reverend William Fox, an amateur fossil hunter, after whom it was named.

In 1882 it was suggested that *Hypsilophodon* was a tree-climbing animal, like a tree kangaroo. More work done in 1974 by P.M. Galton showed that it was not.

Hypsilophodon was a small dinosaur, no more than 2.3 metres (7 feet 6 inches) long.

It was a plant-eater.

This was quite a primitive-looking animal for the time in which it lived. It had the bird-hipped dinosaur's beak, but it also had teeth in the front of its jaw. There were five fingers on the hand and four on the foot. These are all features that we would expect to find on much earlier dinosaurs.

The hypsilophodont group as a whole was a long-lasting one, surviving unchanged from the late Jurassic to the end of the Cretaceous. They did not need to change much during that time because they were so beautifully adapted for the lifestyle that they followed. The whole body was that of a swift runner. It would have browsed amongst low-growing vegetation and taken refuge from predators like *Megalosaurus* or *Baryonyx* by sprinting away into the undergrowth of the forest.

Hypsilophodon was one of the smallest and fastest of the Cretaceous plant-eating dinosaurs.

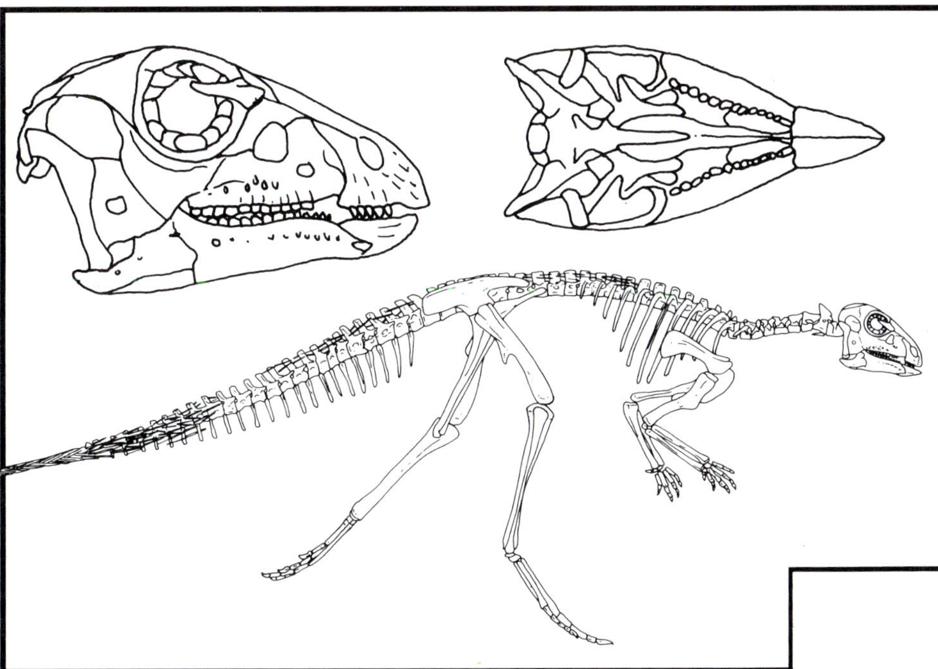

The jaws had teeth at the front as well as a horny beak.

The lightweight body, stiff tail and long legs show *Hypsilophodon* to have been a swift runner.

Most hypsilophodontids were small – no bigger than a man – but one, *Tenontosaurus*, grew to be 6.5 metres (20 feet) long.

IGUANODON MANTELLI

'MANTELL'S IGUANA TOOTH'

ORNITHOPODA, IGUANODONTID

EARLY CRETACEOUS

EUROPE – PARTICULARLY SOUTHERN ENGLAND AND BELGIUM – NORTH AFRICA, WESTERN NORTH AMERICA, MONGOLIA, AND SPITZBERGEN IN THE ARCTIC CIRCLE

Dr Gideon Mantell, after whom the animal was named, and his wife Mary found the first bones and teeth in Sussex, England, in the early 1920s. Mantell published the first description in 1825, but it was not very accurate since there was very little to go on. The teeth were thought to look like those of the modern iguana lizard, hence the name.

The most famous, and extensive, discovery was in a mine at Bernisaart in Belgium in 1878. Thirty-nine skeletons, many of them almost complete, were found in what had once been a ravine. The first account of these was published by Louis Dollo in 1882. Since then, many discoveries have been made. One in Nehden, West Germany, in 1980 prompted a further thorough study by Dr David Norman at Brasenose College, Oxford.

The biggest *Iguanodon* was 9 metres (30 feet long). *Iguanodon* was a plant-eater, probably grazing low-level ferns and horsetails.

The fossil of an animal called *Muttaburrasaurus* was found in Australia in 1981, and another, called *Probactrosaurus*, was found in Asia in 1966. These were both very *Iguanodon*-like and show that the iguanodontids spread throughout almost the whole of the globe in early Cretaceous times. Iguanodontid footprints have been found on Spitzbergen, within the Arctic Circle. Shortly after this time the continents began to break up and move apart. It was the last time that a major group of animals could spread worldwide like this.

▼ The fossilized *Iguanodon* herd at Bernisaart in Belgium shows that this dinosaur moved about in large groups, and that the males and females were of quite different sizes.

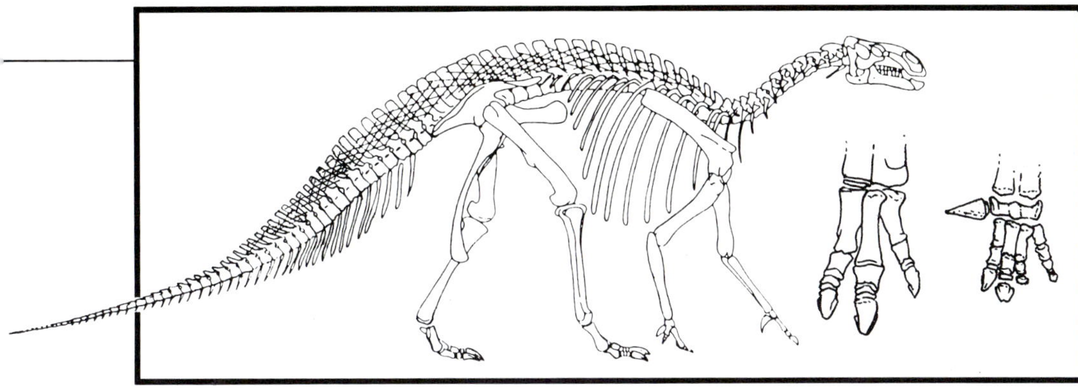

The hand of *Iguanodon* had a big spike on the thumb. This may have been used in defence, food-gathering or mating. The three middle fingers had hooves and were for walking on. They could also be splayed outwards, like a foot. The fifth finger was small and flexible, and acted as a kind of a thumb when feeding.

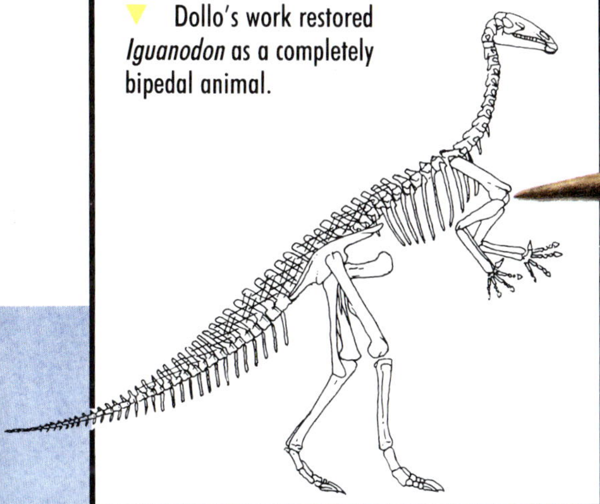

Dollo's work restored *Iguanodon* as a completely bipedal animal.

Early restorations showed *Iguanodon* as a kind of big lizard. The horn on the nose was actually the thumb spike.

Modern restorations have returned the animal to Mantell's four-footed stance.

OURANOSAURUS NIGERIENSIS

'BRAVE MONITOR LIZARD FROM NIGER'
ORNITHOPODA, IGUANODONTID
EARLY CRETACEOUS
WEST AFRICA

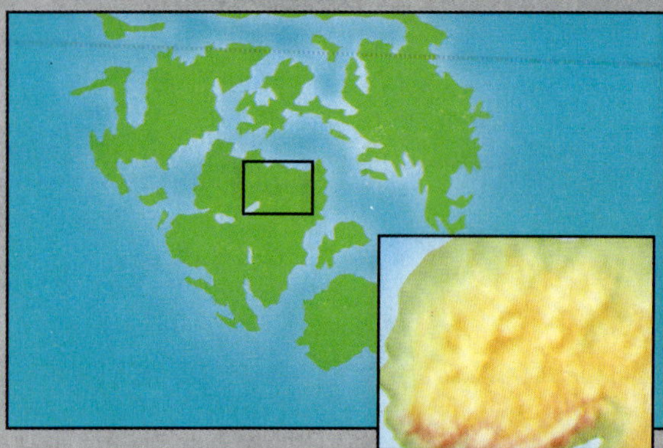

The almost complete skeleton of *Ouranosaurus* was discovered in 1966 by an expedition from the National Museum of Natural History in Paris. The skeleton was mounted and a description published by Dr Philippe Taquet in 1976.

It was 7 metres (23 feet) long.

As with all other iguanodonts, *Ouranosaurus* was a plant-eater.

▶ *Ouranosaurus* lived out in the open, on crocodile-infested river plains.

The obvious difference between *Ouranosaurus* and the other iguanodonts – and indeed the other ornithopods – was the strange structure down its back. The spines of the backbone were extended upwards as a series of planks, like the slats of a fence. In life this fence was probably covered by skin and used by *Ouranosaurus* as a combined solar panel and radiator – warming up the animal when turned to the sun and cooling it when held to the wind. On the other hand, it may have been the basis for a fleshy hump, like we see in present-day North American bison. On the evidence that we have at the moment, the solar panel/radiator seems the more likely. *Spinosaurus* (p. 96–7), from the same area and almost the same period, had a similar structure.

Ouranosaurus was quite a heavy animal. Although it had the typical iguanodontid hand, with the spiky thumb, it evidently spent most of its time on all fours. The legs were quite massive and were not designed for fast running.

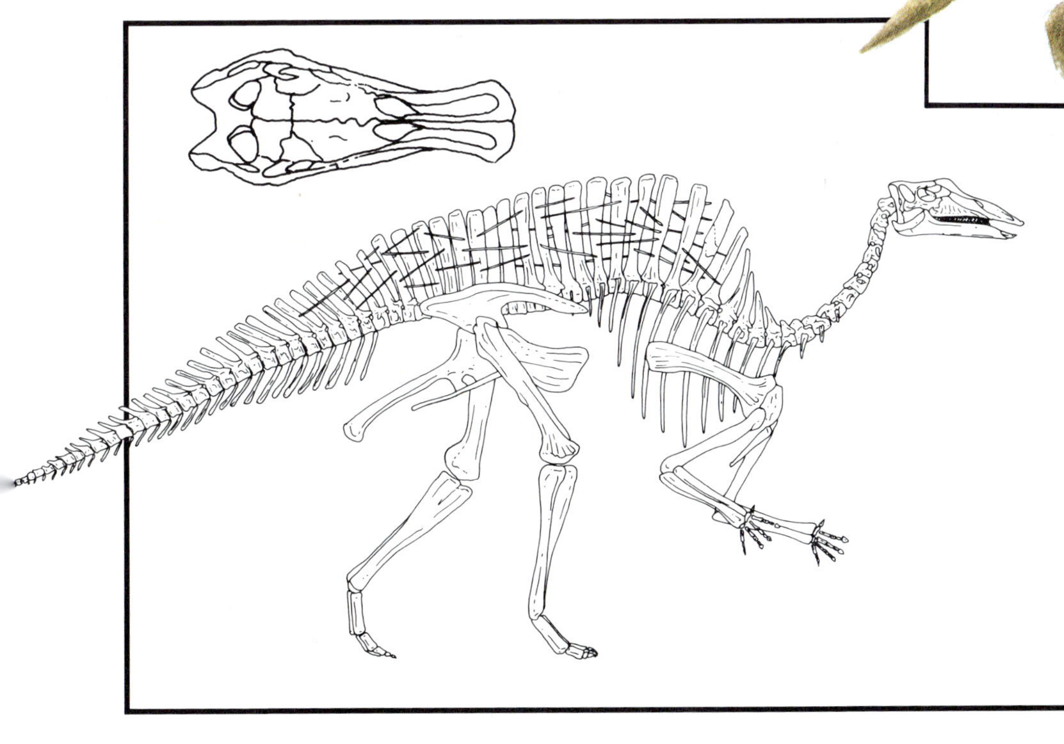

▲ If the back structure did not support a sail, then it must have supported a hump. We do not know which.

◄ The skull was broad and flat, like that of one of the later 'duckbills'. There was a lump, like a small crest, on top.

◄ The body and tail seemed to form a stiff mass. The neck, on the other hand was very flexible.

PSITTACOSAURUS MONGOLIENSIS

'PARROT LIZARD FROM MONGOLIA'
CERATOPSIA, PSITTACOSAURID
EARLY CRETACEOUS
MONGOLIA, AND KANSU AND SHANTUNG IN CHINA

The first two specimens of *Psittacosaurus* were found on the American Museum of Natural History expedition to Mongolia in 1922–5. The first description was published by Henry Fairfield Osborn in 1923.

Other specimens of *Psittacosaurus* were brought back by the expedition, but the American Museum of Natural History did not realize it until 1980. Then it was pointed out, by Walter Coombes, that some small fragments of fossilized bone were actually remains of baby *Psittacosauri.*

The adult *Psittacosaurus* was about 1.5 metres (5 feet) long and would have weighed about 22 kilograms (50 pounds). The babies would have been about 25 centimetres (10 inches) long.

They were plant-eaters.

This, the earliest known of the ceratopsians, was quite unlike its later relatives. It was, in fact, built much more like one of the smaller ornithopods, like *Hypsilophodon* (p. 84–5). So much so, in fact, that many palaeontologists prefer to classify it as one of the lightly-built bird-footed dinosaurs, and not one of the heavy rhinoceros-like horned dinosaurs of the later Cretaceous. It probably shows a stage in the process of the one group evolving out of the other.

Its skeleton is just like that of a small ornithopod – with its short front legs, its narrow hands and its two-footed stance. It is the square-shaped skull that shows the ceratopsian features. The beak at the front of the mouth is very large, and the front teeth have been lost. There is a heavy ridge at the back, supporting the jaw muscles. It is this ridge that later evolved into the ceratopsian frill and neck shield.

Although the psittacosaurid group later evolved into the true ceratopsians, *Psittacosaurus* itself could not have been their ancestor. Some later ceratopsians, such as the primitive *Protoceratops* (p. 120–1), still had their front teeth. These were already lost by *Psittacosaurus*. The later ceratopsians had five fingers on the forelimb. *Psittacosaurus* had only four. *Psittacosaurus* had already gone some way down its own evolutionary path and the ceratopsians evidently branched off some time earlier.

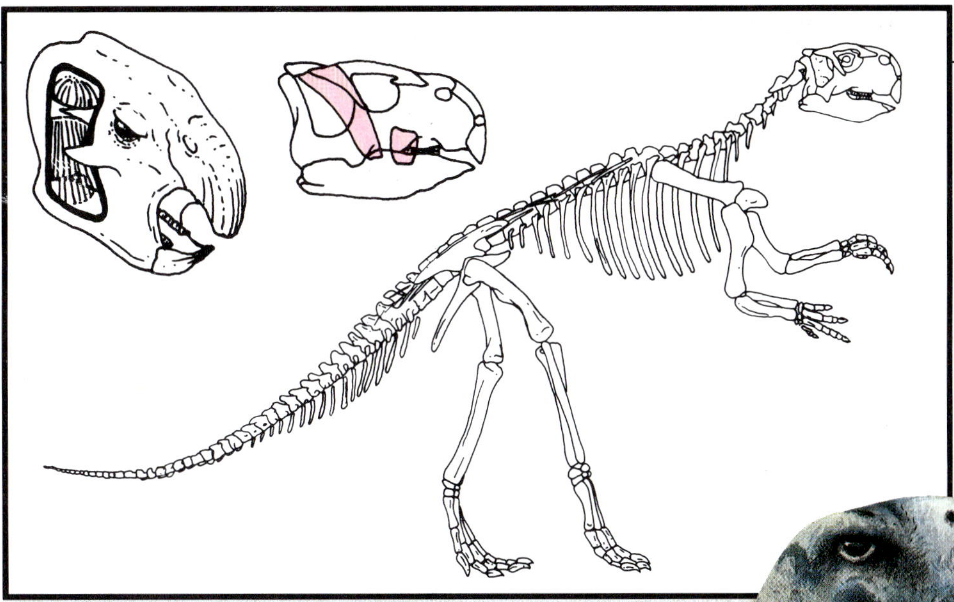

◀ The parrot-liked head of *Psittacosaurus* was produced by the strong beak and the ridge at the back of the skull.

◀ The skull ridge, which later evolved into the ceratopsian frill, supported the powerful jaw muscles.

◀ The skeleton was very much like that of a small ornithopod.

▼ *Psittacosaurus* probably browsed from low plants growing close to the ground.

LATE CRETACEOUS GEOGRAPHY

In the second half of the Cretaceous period, from about 90 million years ago onward, almost all the continents had split away from one another and Pangaea was no more. By the end of the period, 65 million years ago, the only continents that were yet to separate were Australia from Antarctica and Greenland from Scandinavia. Otherwise, they were all heading out towards the positions in which we see them today.

One result of this movement was that the seas flooded over the low-lying lands to an extent to which they had never reached before. The beginning of this rise in sea level – or transgression, as the geologists call it – occurred at the same time the world over. It may be that the separation of the continents threw up huge oceanic ridges at the new plate margins, and these ridges displaced volumes of water over the low-lying continents.

One vast shallow seaway, the Niobrara, stretched north-south along the line of the old Sundance Sea, but separated the Rocky Mountains completely from the rest of the North American continent. Europe, except for Scandinavia, was likewise almost totally submerged. Another sea reached southwards across North Africa, where the Sahara now lies, cutting Africa into two land masses.

Almost the only areas that were not sinking below the sea were the borders of the Pacific ocean – for we can now talk about the Pacific rather than Panthalassa. Here, along the coasts of Australia, eastern Asia and North and South America, mountains and island chains were being thrown up as old ocean floor was swallowed up beneath the spreading continents.

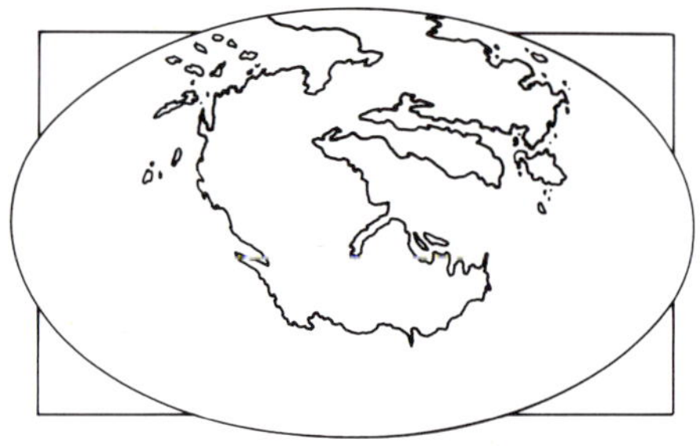

TRIASSIC
215 million years ago

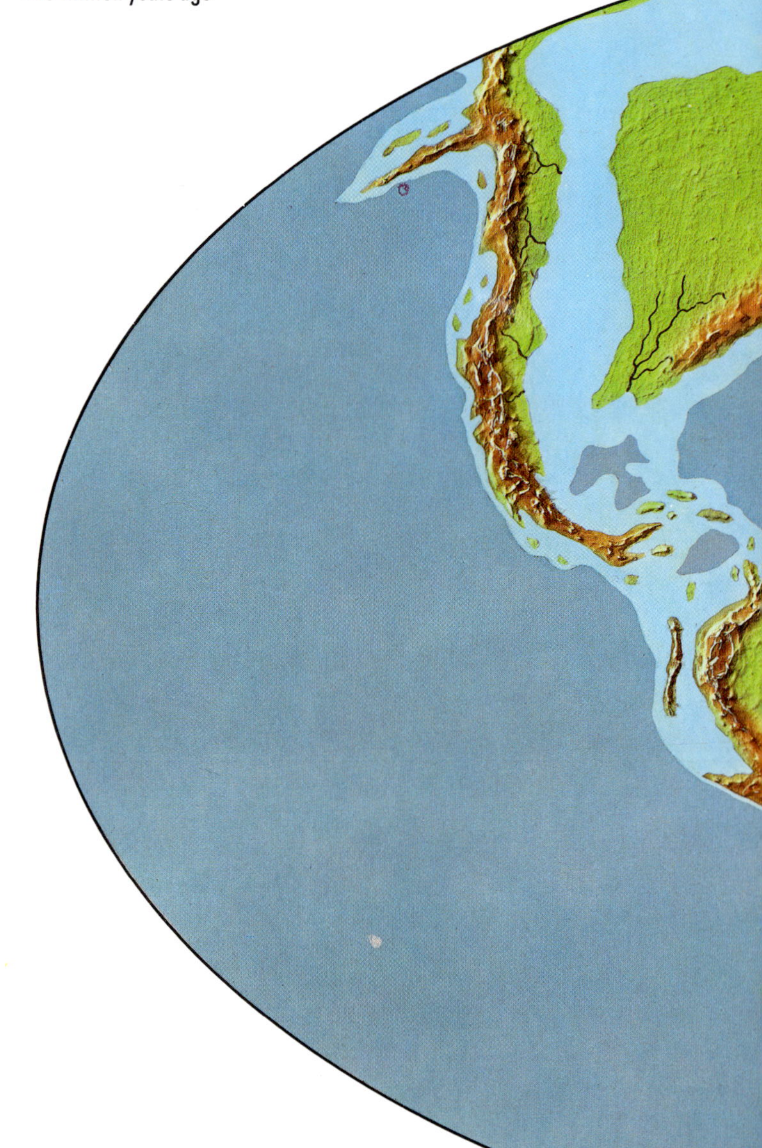

LATE JURASSIC
145 million years ago

By the late Cretaceous, the world was a quite different place from what it had been during the rest of the Mesozoic. Pangaea was gone now, and in its place there were scattered island continents. Panthalassa also no longer existed, since new oceans were growing rapidly between the individual continents. A raising of the sea level, probably produced by all the new oceanic ridges that were being generated, spread shallow seas everywhere over the continental edges and vast areas of continental shelf were flooded.

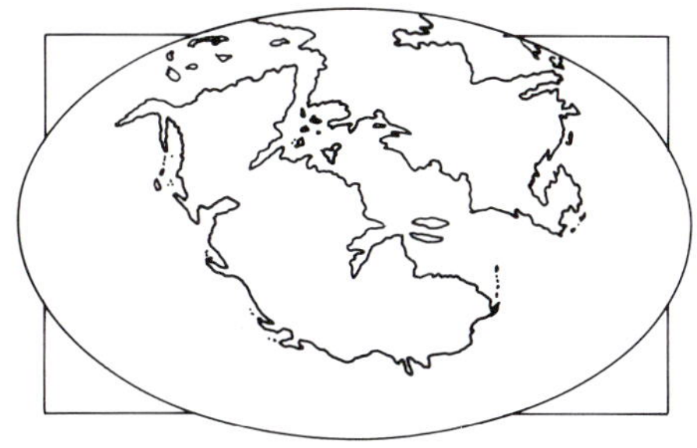

EARLY JURASSIC
180 million years ago

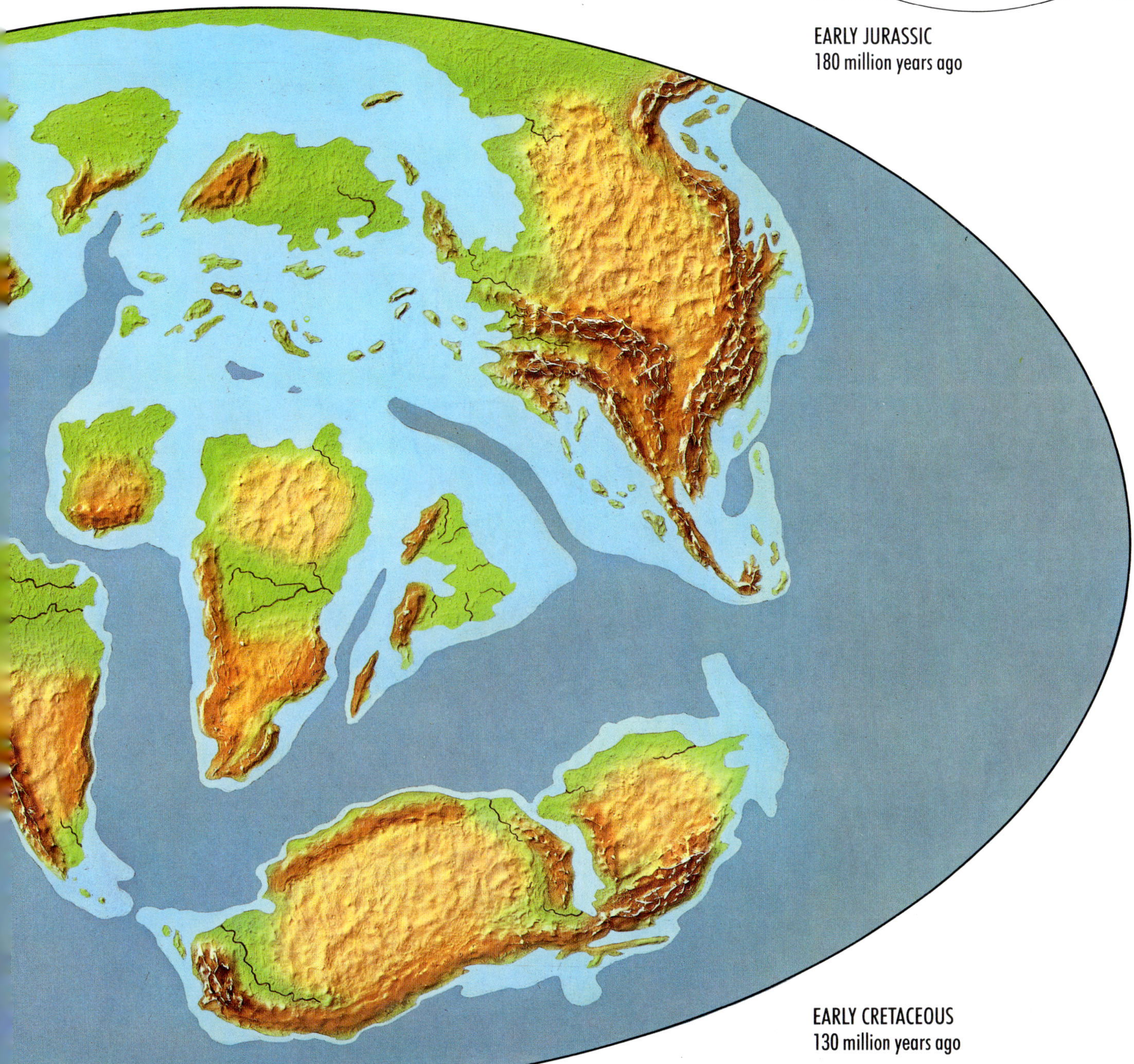

EARLY CRETACEOUS
130 million years ago

LATE CRETACEOUS CONDITIONS

The climates began to cool at last, and for the first time climates varied throughout the world.

Forests of modern plants developed, and North America saw thick woods and forests of willows, oaks, maples, hickory and many other trees that we would recognize today. Cycads were still abundant, however, and there were still no grasses.

Because of the scatter of continents, and the vast areas of shallow seas between, each continent tended to have its own types of animals, just like Australia today has kangaroos and koalas and other animals that evolved only there. From time to time North America was joined to northern Asia across the Bering Straits, and the animal life was very similar in these two areas. Both had the duckbilled dinosaurs, such as *Anatosaurus* (p. 108–9), *Saurolophus* (p. 110–11) and *Parasaurolophus* (p. 112–3), and the big and small meat-eaters, like *Tyrannosaurus* (p. 98–9), *Ornithominus* (p. 100–1) and *Saurornithoides* (p. 104–5).

Dry areas still existed in Mongolia, where *Protoceratops* (p. 120–1) and *Velociraptor*

▲ The late Cretaceous forests of North America were quite unlike any that existed during the rest of the Mesozoic. Indeed, they were very similar to, and contained the same plants as, many of the forests of today. This did not have much effect on the dinosaurs, who were able to adapt to the new vegetation.

▲ Some continental interiors were still quite dry. The largest known pterosaur, *Quetzalcoatlus*, soared in the sky above what is now southern North America. The dry open plains that existed here would have provided rising masses of warm air that would have supported such huge animals.

▼ The Niobrara sea of central North America produced vast deposits of chalk that are now found in Kansas. In the sea lived long-necked plesiosaurs, like *Elasmosaurus*, mosasaurs, like *Tylosaurus*, and early sea birds, like *Ichthyornis* and the flightless *Hesperornis*.

(p. 102–3) lived, and in north Africa, where *Spinosaurus* (p. 96–7) hunted. In the mountains of North America there lived armoured dinosaurs like *Stegoceras* (p. 114–5), *Euoplocephalus* (p. 116–7), *Panoplosaurus* (p. 118–9), *Chasmosaurus* (p. 122–3), *Styracosaurus* (p. 124–5) and *Triceratops* (p. 126–7).

These creatures did not reach some of the other continents. The duckbills were plentiful in North America and Asia but were not at all common in South America. Instead, the long-necked plant-eaters, such as *Saltasaurus* (p. 106–7) lived on in that continent.

Pterosaurs cruised the skies, some of them, like *Pteranodon*, fishing like albatrosses in the vast new shallow seas. Others lived inland, probably feeding on carrion, such as *Quetzalcoatlus*, the size of a small aeroplane and the biggest flying creature known.

In the oceans the plesiosaurs became very long-necked, as in *Elasmosaurus*. The mosasaurs reached a great size: *Tylosaurus*, with the length of a small boat, must have been the most ferocious sea reptile that ever existed.

SPINOSAURUS AEGIPTICUS

'EGYPTIAN SPINED LIZARD'
THEROPODA, SPINOSAURID
LATE CRETACEOUS
NORTH AFRICA

Spinosaurus was first described in 1915 by Stromer, from bits and pieces found near Baharije in Egypt.

The original remains were lost during World War II. Other remains have been found in Niger, Africa.

Spinosaurus was a very large animal, reaching lengths of about 12 metres (40 feet).

The spines on its back were up to 1.8 metres (6 feet) long and rather club-shaped.

Could anything be more impressive than a massive meat-eating dinosaur – one of the biggest that ever lived – sporting a huge sail on its back? Our amazement at this back ornament may throw some light on its function. If we are amazed at the mere thought of it, think of the effect it would have had on the other animals of the time! It might have been a warning sign, to tell other animals to keep away. It might have been a brightly-coloured flag to attract a mate, like a peacock's tail.

On the other hand, the sail may have acted like a radiator. *Spinosaurus* may have lived in a very hot climate. If it did, it may have built up a great deal of body heat during the activities of the day. A sail like this, held to the wind, would have cooled the animal's blood. Conversely, the sail, held up to the early morning sun, would have warmed the blood after the chilly night and enabled the *Spinosaurus* to become active and to go hunting earlier than other animals.

This heat-radiator explanation may be the correct one. Unrelated plant-eating dinosaurs, such as *Ouranosaurus* (p. 88–9), living in the scorching climate of North Africa at about this time, also had sails like this.

▶ A sail held to the sun in the morning would have warmed the animal. The sail held to catch the wind in the heat of the day would have cooled it.

The sail may have been brightly coloured to act as some sort of a signal.

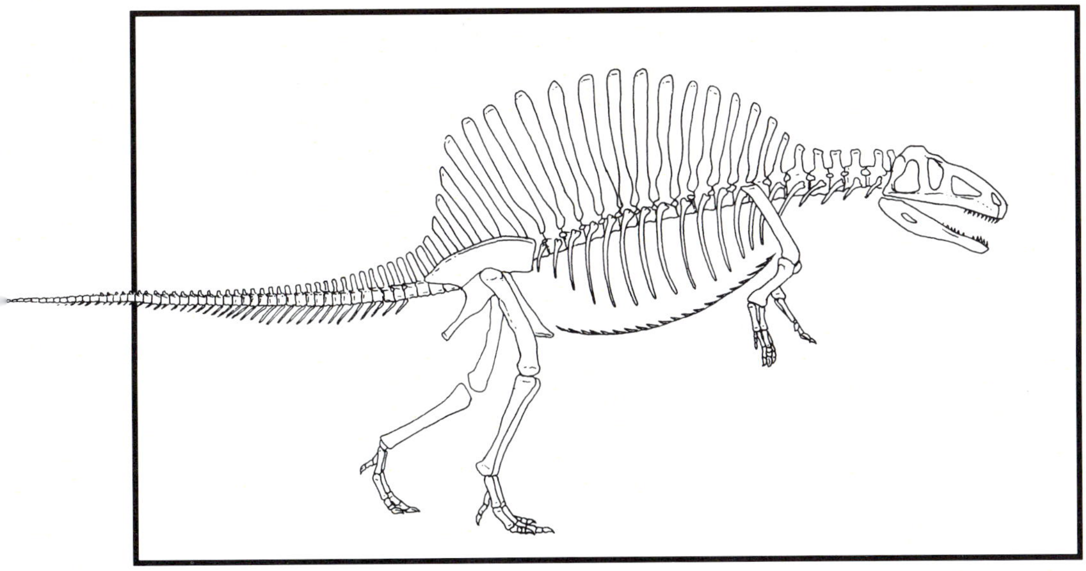

◀ Except for the sail, *Spinosaurus* was built like any other big meat-eating dinosaur. The meat-slicing teeth were straight, rather than curved as in other meat-eaters.
The forelimbs were larger than those of similar animals.
The sail was supported by spines growing upwards from each back vertebra.

▶ There were several spinosaurs, but the other members of the group had much lower spines on their backs. *Altispinax* (1), from the early Cretaceous of southern England, was typical.
Other animals throughout time had sails on their backs. *Dimetrodon* (2) was a carnivorous reptile, and *Platyhystrix* (3) a land-living amphibian, both from the Permian of Texas, USA.

TYRANNOSAURUS REX

'KING TYRANT LIZARD'
THEROPODA, TYRANNOSAURID
LATE CRETACEOUS
NORTH AMERICA

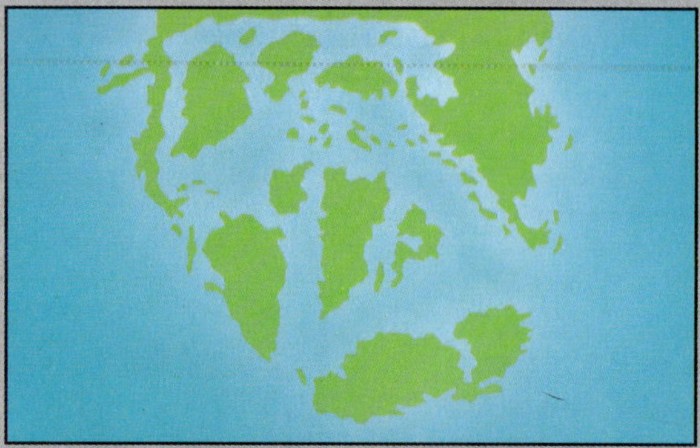

This great dinosaur was first described and named by Henry Fairfield Osborn in 1905 from a partial skeleton discovered in 1902 by the fossil collector Barnum Brown in Montana, USA. Since then, many partial skeletons have been found, but not a single one has been complete.

Only parts of the tail have ever been discovered, and so there has been much argument about the total length. But *Tyrannosaurus* is thought to have been about 12 metres (40 feet) long and weighed 6 tons.

Tyrannosaurus ate meat.

Tyrannosaurus with its huge muscular jaws, its teeth like saw-edged scimitars, its strong flexible neck and its powerful hind legs, was the mightiest killer that ever walked. Crashing out of the jungle it could have thundered down on the biggest animals alive at the time and killed them quickly and savagely with great tearing bites and slashes. What a monster!

But was it such a monster? Doubts arose in the 1960s when studies seemed to show that the hips of *Tyrannosaurus* would only have allowed the animal to take small, mincing steps and move at only about 5 kilometres per hour (3 mph). The huge teeth were definitely for tearing up meat, but what kind of meat? Probably just the rotting carcasses of dead animals. Mighty *Tyrannosaurus* was just a scavenger!

Since the 1960s, however, scientific opinion has turned the other way. The eyes of *Tyrannosaurus* could be directed forward to give a three-dimensional view past its narrow nose. Only active hunters can do this. The teeth were strong enough to grip struggling prey. The feet had small claws and few heavy muscles – these are adaptations for speed. The skull and the powerful jaw muscles were designed to withstand the impact of the 6-tonne body crashing into the flank of an unsuspecting hadrosaur at a speed of 30 kilometres per hour (20 mph). So, *Tyrannosaurus* could really have been a swift and deadly hunter, rather than a placid scavenger, after all.

Scientists have reached a compromise: it was both a fast hunter *and* a scavenger.

▶ *Tyrannosaurus* prowled the late Cretaceous forests of North America, either killing hadrosaurs or feeding on carcasses.

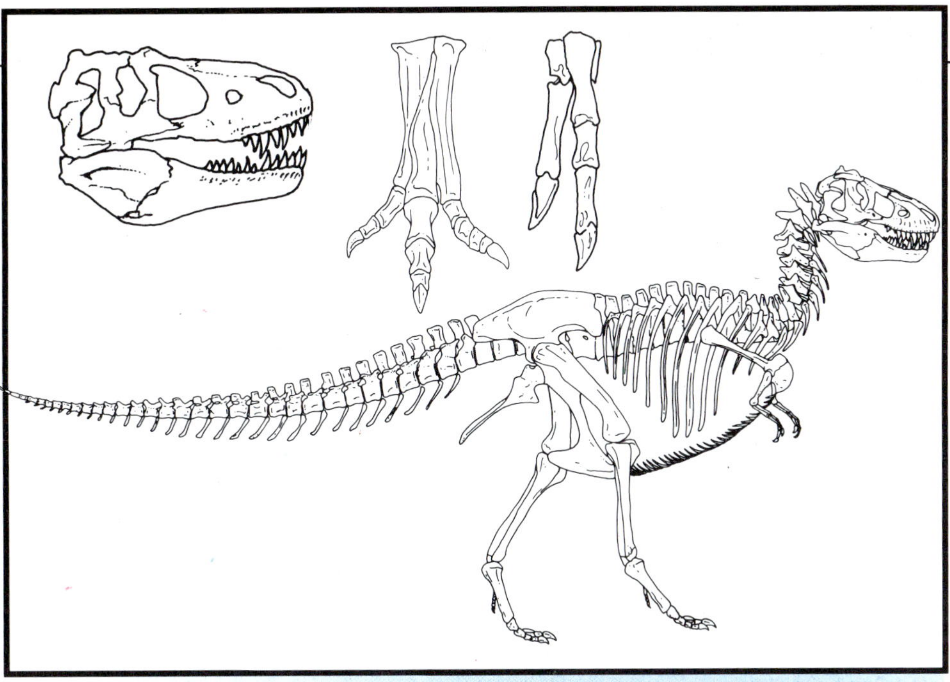

The skull of *Tyrannosaurus* was short and deep, with huge teeth of different sizes. The perforations in the skull by the teeth would have carried blood vessels and nerves to muscular lips.

The strong hips and the belly ribs show that *Tyrannosaurus* spent much of its time lying down.

The silly little arms with the two-fingered hand were probably used for helping *Tyrannosaurus* to rise to its feet.

ORNITHOMIMUS VELOX

'FAST BIRD MIMIC'
THEROPODA, ORNITHOMIMID
LATE CRETACEOUS
COLORADO AND MONTANA, USA

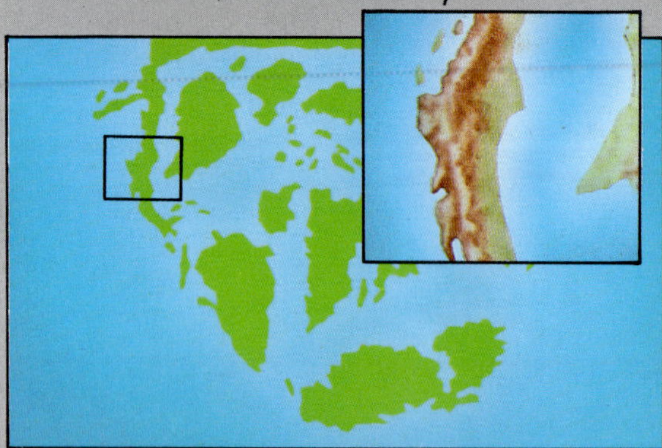

Ornithomimids lived in the swampy floodplains between the Rocky Mountains and the Sundance Sea.

Ornithomimus was the first of the ostrich-like dinosaurs to be discovered. The first remains were some foot bones discovered near Denver, Colorado, by George Cannon in 1889. Othniel Marsh gave them the name *Ornithomimus*. It was not until 1917, when an almost complete skeleton was described by Henry Fairfield Osborn, that scientists knew what an ostrich-like dinosaur was really like. This was the skeleton of the closely related *Struthiomimus*.

Ornithomimus was about 3.5 metres (11½ feet) long but, with the proportions of an ostrich, it had quite a small body.

Ornithomimus probably foraged close to the ground, pecking at low plants and ground-living animals. On the other hand it may have been an egg-stealer, or it may even have fed on shoots and twigs from the tops of bushes.

The bird-mimics are well named, not because they could fly (they couldn't), but because they were built like the modern flightless birds – the ostriches, emus and cassowaries. They must have been among the most graceful and elegant of the dinosaurs. Their compact bodies were supported on stilt-like legs and they had a very small head and long neck. Like birds, they even lacked teeth.

It is obvious from their build that all bird-mimics were running animals. The hind legs were built for running, with all the muscles concentrated at the thigh. Tendons ran down the legs and worked the foot bones. There were only three toes – the small third toe that most theropods possessed was missing in *Ornithomimus*. This helped to produce a lightweight running foot. The ornithomimids were obviously able to sprint away very quickly from any danger.

▼ If the ornithomimids ate twigs, they could easily reach the tops of bushes with their long necks and long clawed hands.

▶ The jaws had no teeth, but were probably covered by a bird-like beak. The eye was quite large and supported by a ring of bone.

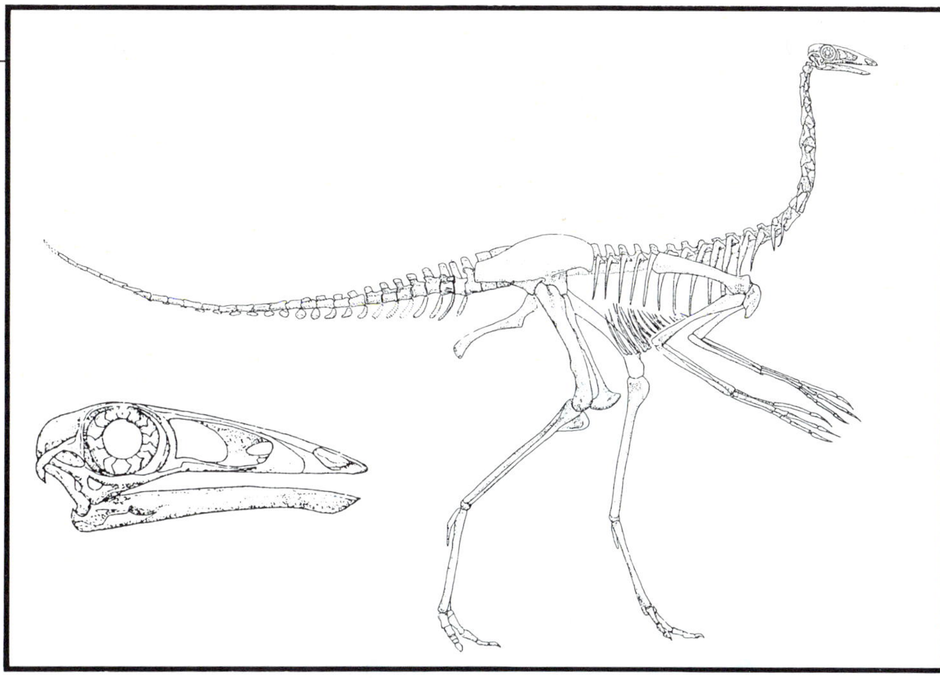

▼ If the ornithomimids ate buried dinosaur eggs, they would have been able to uncover them by scraping away at the soil with their hands and peck into them with their beaks. If an angered parent appeared, they would have been able to sprint away quickly.

▲ Some ornithomimids lived on the open plains, but *Ornithomimus* itself was a forest-dweller, living in the cypress swamps of late Cretaceous North America.

VELOCIRAPTOR MONGOLIENSIS

'MONGOLIAN FAST HUNTER'
THEROPODA, DROMAEOSAURID
LATE CRETACEOUS
MONGOLIA

Velociraptor was first described in 1924 by Henry Fairfield Osborn. The first specimen was one of the many dinosaurs brought back by the American Museum of Natural History's Central Asiatic Expedition – an expedition that went to look for fossil man, but found dinosaurs instead. A much better specimen was found in 1971 by the Polish-Mongolian Palaeontological Expedition.

Velociraptor was about 1.8 metres (6 feet) long, with a head measuring 15.5 centimetres (6 inches).

An overwhelming piece of evidence suggests that *Velociraptor* ate the horned dinosaur *Protoceratops* (p. 120–1).

With the discovery of *Deinonychus* (p. 82–3), and its publication in 1969, all sorts of earlier fossil finds began to make sense. We were able to see how other problematical creatures fitted into the scheme of things. One of these was *Velociraptor*. No one knew if this small animal was a large version of the small meat-eaters or a small version of the larger ones. It was now evident that *Velociraptor*, *Deinonychus* and other creatures, such as *Dromaeosaurus*, after which the group is named, belonged to a special family of medium-sized hunters. What is more, this family consisted of very active and ferocious beasts that roamed the Cretaceous landscape in packs, hunting for prey.

There is spectacular first-hand evidence of how these animals killed. Imagine if you tickled a cat on its belly. The cat will grasp your hand with its forepaws and try to tear it with the claws of its hind feet. A fossil of the horned *Protoceratops* was found in Mongolia in 1971 with a *Velociraptor* attached to its head shield and behaving in a very cat-like manner. The shield was grasped with the long fingers of the hand, and the hind claws were tearing into the underside of the *Protoceratops* with evident ferocity. For some reason, both animals died in the attack and they were fossilized in that position to this day.

▶ *Velociraptor* probably sprinted about among the sand dunes of late Cretaceous central Asia, hunting in packs for more slow-moving plant-eaters.

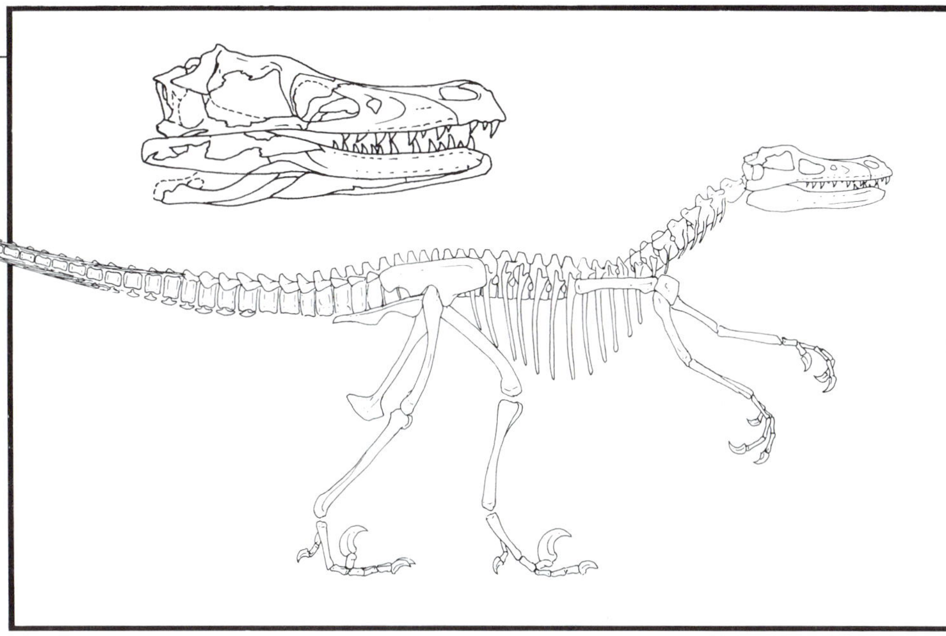

▶ *Velociraptor* had collar bones – something very unusual amongst the dinosaurs. This would have given strength to the grasp of the forelimbs.

▼ *Velociraptor* was rather similar to its larger cousin, *Deinonychus*, except for its low, flattened head.

▶ The skeletons of *Velociraptor* and *Protoceratops*, apparently throttling the life out of one another, show us that life-and-death struggles did occur amongst the dinosaurs.

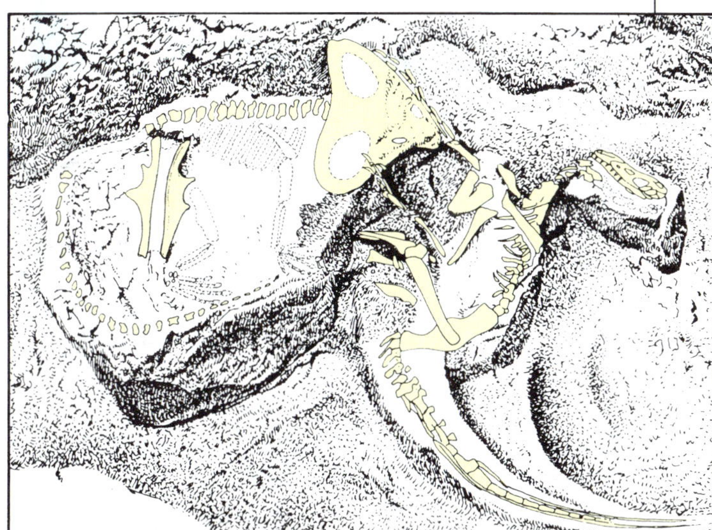

SAURORNITHOIDES MONGOLIENSIS

'MONGOLIAN BIRD-LIKE REPTILE'
THEROPODA, SAURORNITHOIDID
LATE CRETACEOUS
MONGOLIA

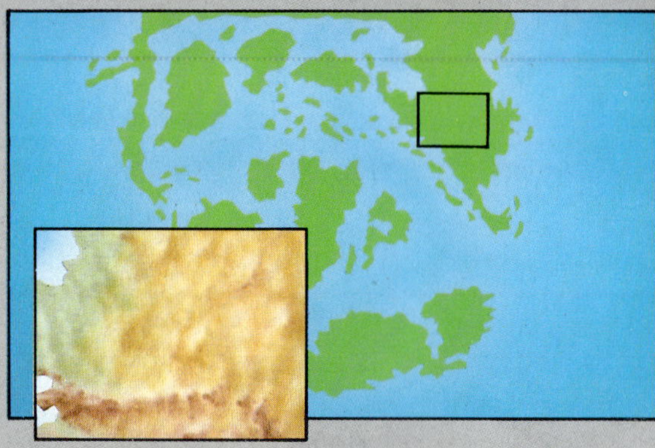

Mongolia was arid desert then, just as it is now.

Saurornithoides was described by Henry Fairfield Osborn in 1924 from incomplete remains found on the famous Central Asiatic Expedition of the American Museum of Natural History. *Saurornithoides* was 2 metres (6½ feet) long, and weighed between 27 and 45 kilograms (60 and 100 lbs).

A very similar saurornithoidid, *Stenonychosaurus*, was discovered in 1932 in Alberta, Canada. The fossil contained only 15 per cent of the bones of the skeleton. Some palaeontologists think that the *Stenonychosaurus* and *Saurornithoides* are the same animal.

The saurornithoidids were so intelligent that Canadian palaeontologist Dale Russell suggested they may have evolved into a human form had they survived to the present day.

It was a meat-eater.

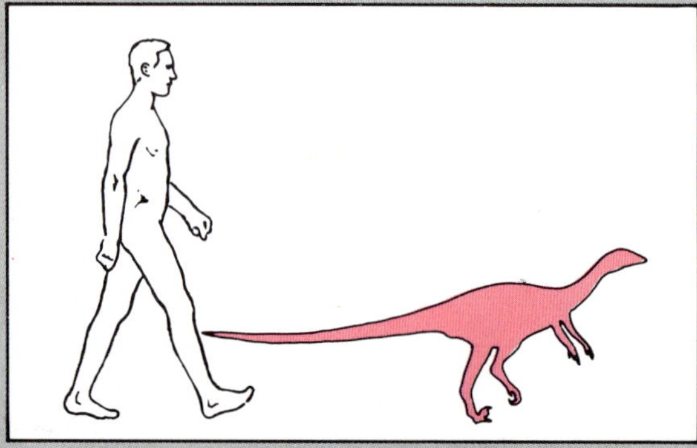

The saurornithoidids had a killing claw on the foot. This was smaller than the killing claw of the dromaeosaurs.

The saurornithoidids appear to have been a group of very intelligent and bird-like dinosaurs. The size of the brain seems to show that they were about as brainy as modern emus, and certainly more intelligent than any modern reptiles. This brain power would have helped them to coordinate their actions when hunting, especially when hunting small active animals like the Mesozoic mammals at dusk. It would also have meant that they could look after their families, probably shepherding their youngsters along, just like ostriches and emus do today.

Saurornithoides and the other saurornithoidids were closely related to the sickle-clawed dromaeosaurs, like *Deinonychus* (p. 82–3). Both groups had a killing claw on the foot and hands that could grasp and hold things. However, in the saurornithoidids the sickle-claw was not nearly so well developed and the tail was not stiffened in the same way.

The skeleton was very lightly-built, just like the other small meat-eating dinosaurs. In fact, some odd bits of bone found in eastern Europe, that were once thought to have belonged to Mesozoic birds, are now thought to have come from saurornithoidids.

▲ *Saurornithoides* and its relatives probably hunted small mammals at dusk.

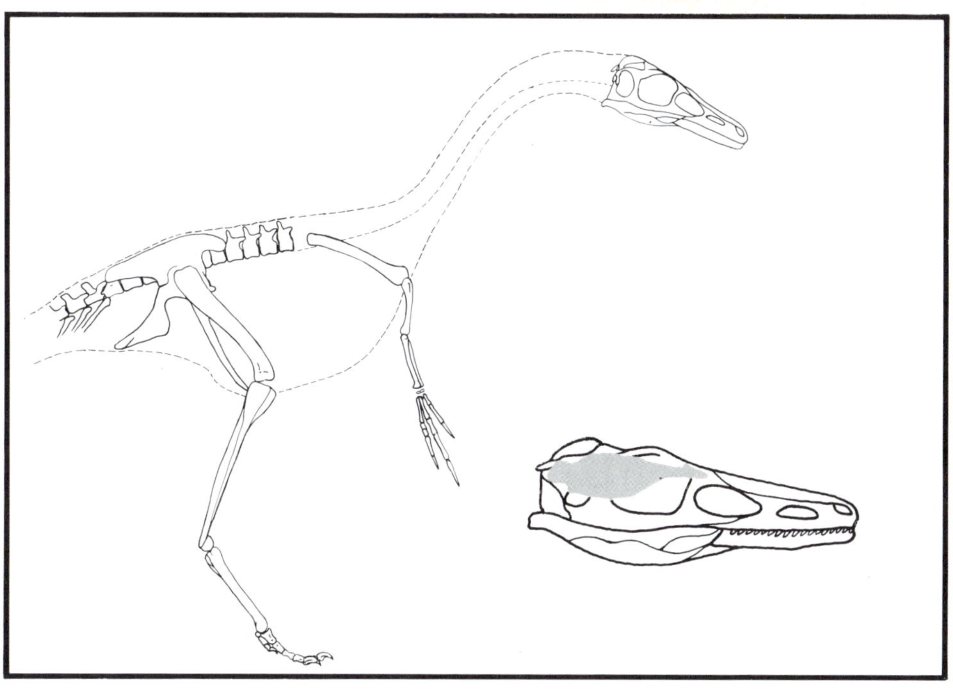

◀ Complete skeletons of *Saurornithoides* have not been found, but the first find consisted of the skull, the hips, part of the backbone and the limbs. This is enough to give us an idea of what the animal looked like.

◀ The very large eyes were widely set and could be directed forward, like those of owls, so that they could see in three dimensions. They had a very large brain as dinosaurs go. They had many teeth, with saw-like rear edges.

SALTASAURUS LORICATUS

'LIZARD FROM SALTA WITH CHAIN MAIL'
SAUROPODOMORPHA, SAUROPOD
LATE CRETACEOUS
ARGENTINA

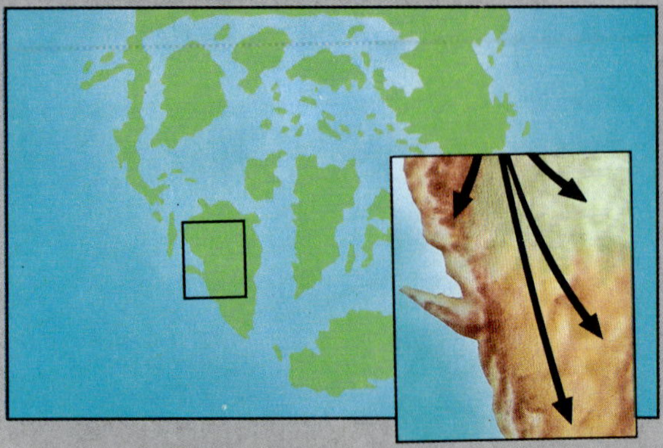

South America in the late Cretaceous was an island continent. Sauropods flourished there, after they had declined or become extinct elsewhere, because of the spread of the duckbills, who were more efficient eaters and deprived the sauropods of food.

This sauropod first came to light in 1980 and was described and named by José Bonaparte and Jaime Powell.

It was named after Salta, the province of north-western Argentina where the remains were discovered.

Saltasaurus was not as large as most other sauropods, reaching a length of about 12 metres (40 feet).

As with all sauropods, and as with all armoured dinosaurs, *Saltasaurus* ate plants.

Like the diplodocids *Saltasaurus* could probably rear up on to its hind legs to reach up into the trees.

The discovery of *Saltasaurus* in 1980 put, as it were, the *Ornitholestes* amongst the pterosaurs! Until that time it was believed that all armoured dinosaurs were ornithischians, like the stegosaurs and the ankylosaurs. It was also believed that the sheer size of the sauropods was enough to defend them against meat-eating creatures. Now, with the discovery of this incredible beast in Argentina, here was a sauropod that was armoured. Apart from this, *Saltasaurus* seemed quite an ordinary sauropod, related more to the diplodocids than the brachiosaurids.

As soon as it was understood that sauropods could have been armoured, the palaeontologists began to take a closer look at other armour remains. Several pieces of armour, that were thought to belong to ankylosaurs, now looked as though they might be parts of sauropods. Indeed, one dinosaur, *Titanosaurus*, discovered and described as a sauropod back in 1893, was later reclassified as an ankylosaur when bits of armour were found with the bones. Now it could be a sauropod again.

South America was an island continent in the late Cretaceous. It formed a sort of a 'Lost World', with sauropods surviving there although they had become extinct on other continents. In most other places they had been replaced as the main tree-eating animals by the duckbills (p. 108–113). But the duckbills never gained a foothold in South America and the sauropods hung on there until the last. It was amongst these late sauropods that the armoured types developed.

Except for the armour, the skeleton of *Saltasaurus* was quite similar to that of any *Diplodocus*-like sauropod.

The armour consisted of a tight mosaic of tiny studs and a number of saucer-sized plates. The plates probably supported horny spikes.

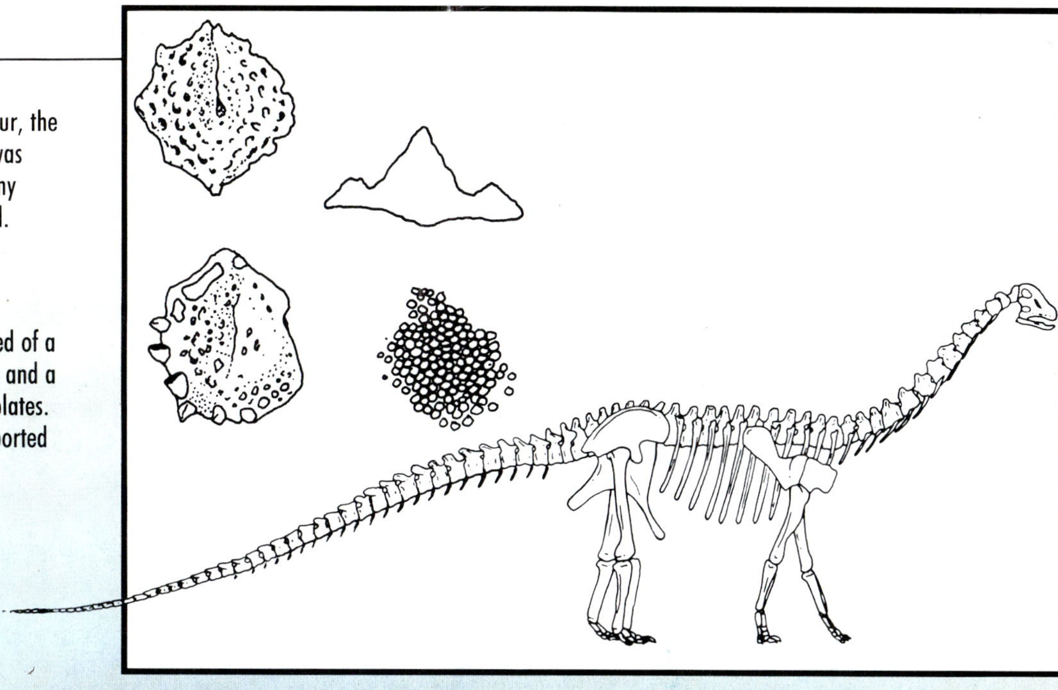

Laplatasaurus, another Argentinian sauropod from the late Cretaceous, used to be restored like this. Now we know that it probably had armour, like *Saltasaurus*.

ANATOSAURUS COPEI

'COPE'S DUCK LIZARD'
ORNITHOPODA, HADROSAURID
LATE CRETACEOUS
NORTH AMERICA

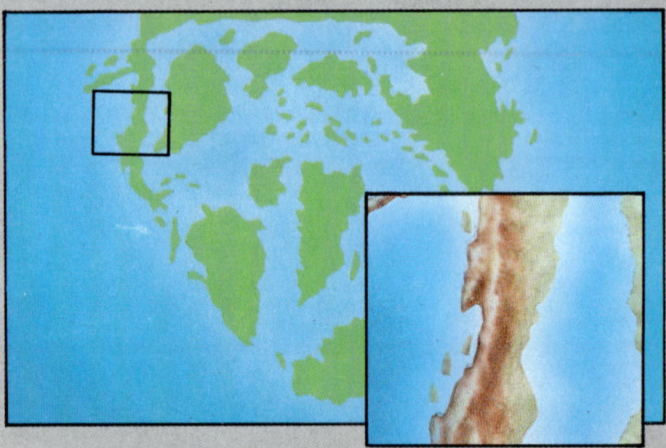

The hadrosaurs were the first dinosaurs to be identified in North America. Joseph Leidy discovered the first – *Hadrosaurus* itself – in 1858. The best specimens of the closely related *Anatosaurus* were found in 1908 by Charles Hazelius Sternberg and his three sons, working for the palaeontologist Edward Drinker Cope. The most significant work on this animal was published by Lull and Wright in 1942.

A fully grown *Anatosaurus* was 9 metres (30 feet) long.

Remains of conifer needles, seeds and twigs have been found in the stomach areas of well-preserved *Anatosaurus* skeletons. The animal evidently browsed from trees.

The hardrosaurs are called the duckbilled dinosaurs. This is because of the shape of the head, and not because of any swimming lifestyle. The front of the skull was broadened into a wide duck-like beak for snipping leaves and twigs. The back of the mouth was not at all duck-like and consisted of several thousand grinding teeth. This equipment enabled *Anatosaurus* to grind up the toughest plant material in its cheek pouches and make a living browsing the trees of the tropical forest in which it lived.

The *Anatosaurus* remains of 1908 were remarkable in that they showed fossilized skin. When the animals died their skins must have dried out very quickly and left an impression in the mud that buried them. From these impressions we can see that the skin was scaly and leathery, and that the muscle of the thigh was contained within the skin of the body.

The legs would have appeared to grow out of the body at the knee, rather than at the hip. The legs and feet were very powerful and the hands had hooves on two of the fingers as well as weight-bearing pads. *Anatosaurus* must have spent much of its time on all fours, although it was basically built as a two-footed animal.

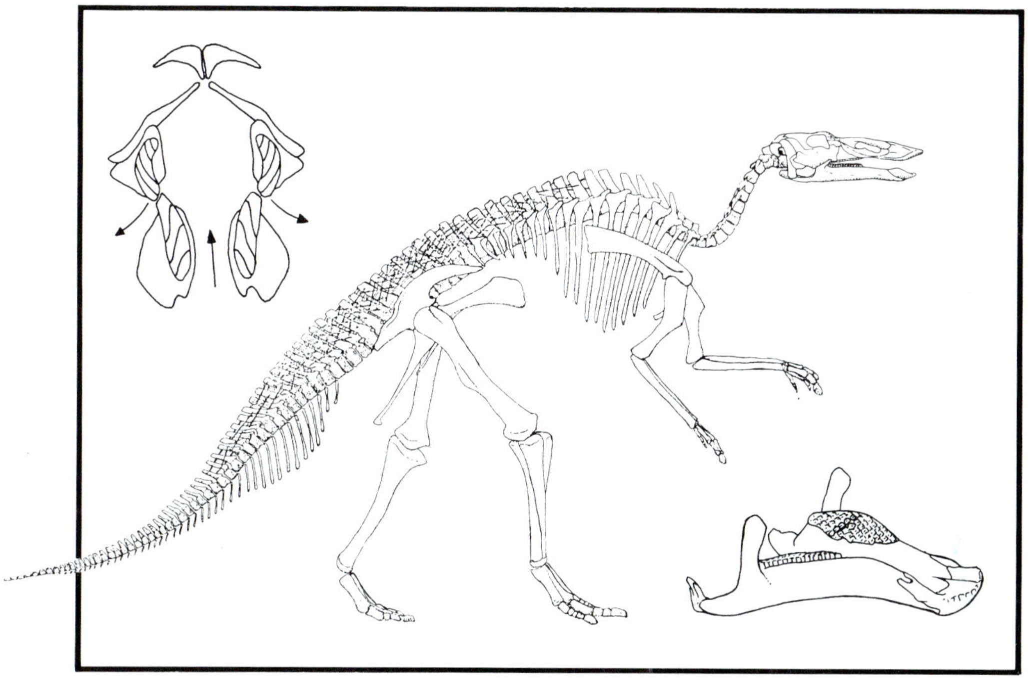

The skeletons of the hadrosaurids were very much like those of the iguanodontids. The downward curve of the shoulders shows that they must have eaten food close to the ground.

The teeth were tightly packed in the jaw and constantly growing, new ones coming up to replace worn old ones. The bones of the upper jaw moved outwards as the lower jaw came up, so that the upper teeth could grind against the lower.

Anatosaurus was a browser of undergrowth and branches in coniferous forests.

The skin was leathery and scaly.

SAUROLOPHUS OSBORNI

'OSBORN'S RIDGED LIZARD'
ORNITHOPODA, HARDROSAURID
LATE CRETACEOUS
ALBERTA, CANADA, AND MONGOLIA

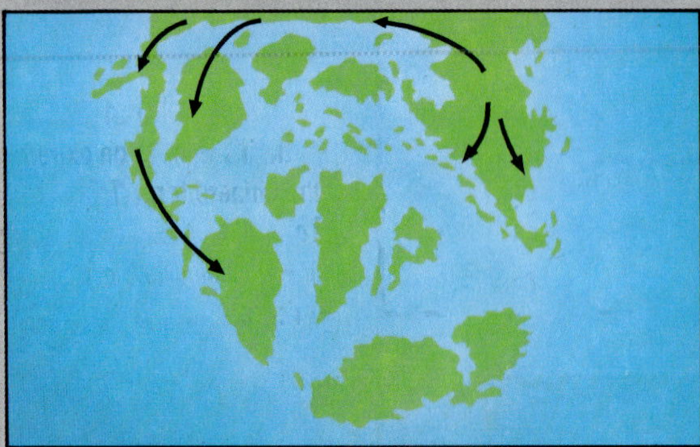

Saurolophus osborni was first described from a complete skeleton found in Canada in 1912 by the famed dinosaur collector Barnum Brown, working for the American Museum of Natural History. Brown's success on this expedition embarrassed the Canadian authorities and spurred them on to their own dinosaur hunts. Another species, *S. angustirostris,* was found in Mongolia in 1952.

The interchange of duckbills between Asia and North America shows that the two continents were connected at that time. Duckbills never gained a real foothold anywhere else, probably because the other continents were drifting away by that time.

Brown named his discovery after Henry Fairfield Osborn, his superior in the American Museum of Natural History.

S. osborni measured 9 metres (30 feet), but the Asian *S. angustirostris* was 12 metres (40 feet) long.

Like the rest of the duckbills, *Saurolophus* was a forest browser.

Although many of the duckbilled dinosaurs were flat-headed, others had crests on their heads. The crests were either hollow and made up of the nose passages, or else they were solid lumps and spikes of bone. *Saurolophus* was typical of the solid-crested type.

The crests were probably used as signalling structures. They made the animal's appearance different from that of other duckbills. The flat-headed and solid-crested duckbills probably also had flaps of skin on their broad snouts above their nostrils. These would have been inflated as the animal breathed, and would have allowed it to give out a tremendous bellow when it wanted to signal. Today frogs, elephant seals and even elephants use their soft breathing apparatus to make signalling noises in the same way. In the case of the solid-crested duckbills, the crest could have served as a support for these sounding bellows.

Between 1979 and 1982, a remarkable discovery was made in Montana, USA – a whole rookery of dinosaur nests! Each nest was about 3 metres (10 feet) in diameter and 1.5 metres (5 feet) high. The eggs were laid in a crater 2 metres (6 feet 6 inches) wide and .75 metres (2 feet 6 inches) deep in the summit. Each nest was about 7 metres (23 feet) from its neighbour. They had been made of mud, like modern flamingo's nests. The animal that made them was *Maiasaura* – a solid-crested duckbill rather like *Saurolophus*. Many youngsters were found in the nests at all stages of growth, showing that there was some form of family structure. Parent duckbills looked after their young. However, that did not prevent their entire colony from perishing and becoming fossilized.

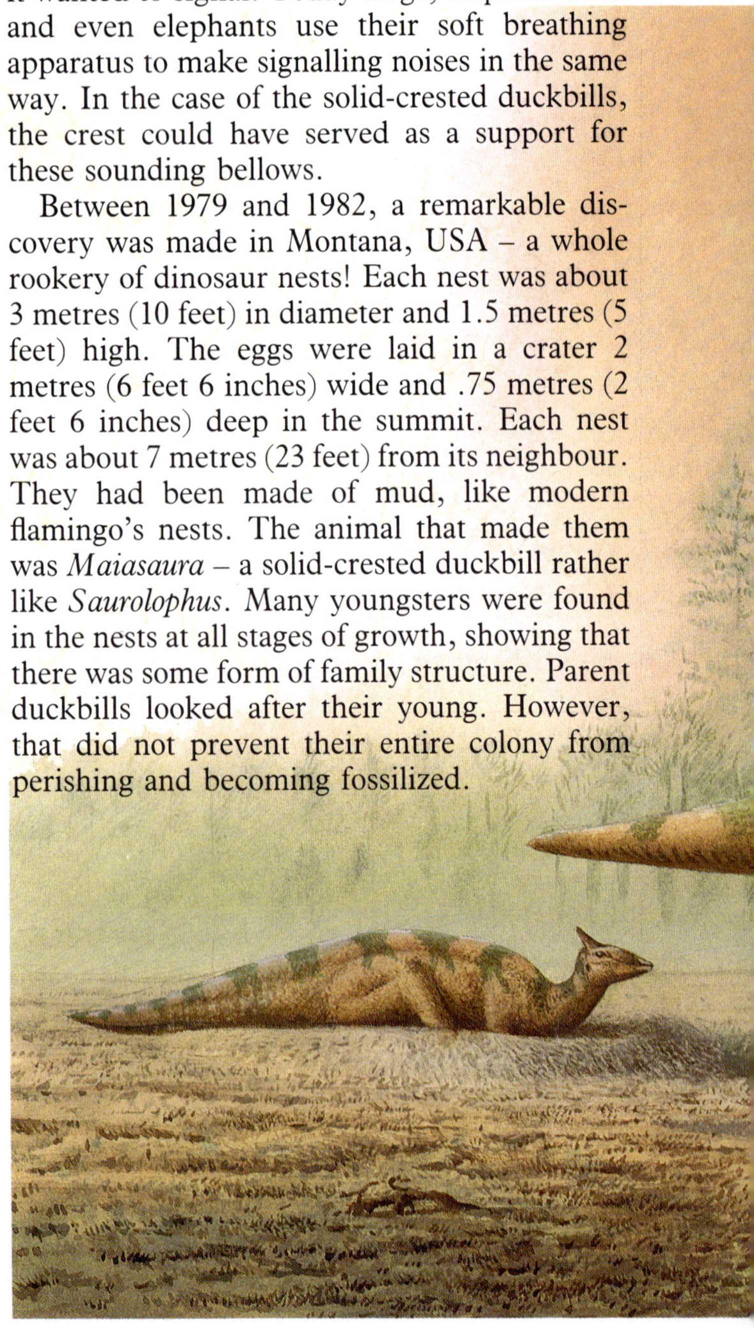

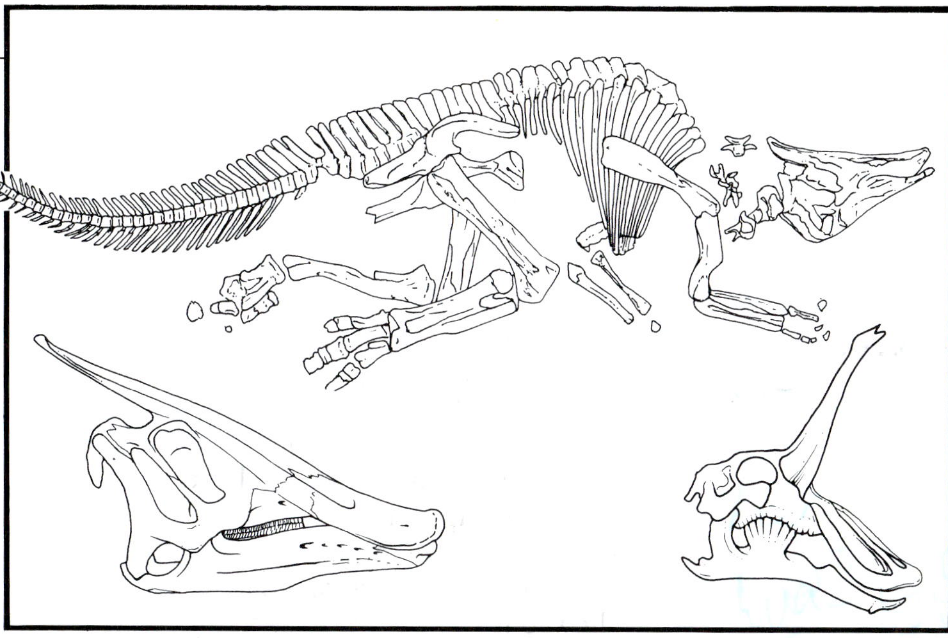

The skeletons of *Saurolophus*, and of the other solid-crested duckbills, were very similar to those of the flat-headed duckbills.

The solid-crests of the duckbills went to an extreme in the Chinese form *Tsintaosaurus.* This had a great spike jutting upwards like the horn of a unicorn.

Duckbills like *Saurolophus* nested together in herds, looking after their young until they were ready to take care of themselves.

A flap of skin above the nostrils may have allowed the flat-headed and solid-crested duckbills to bellow messages to one another and to enemies.

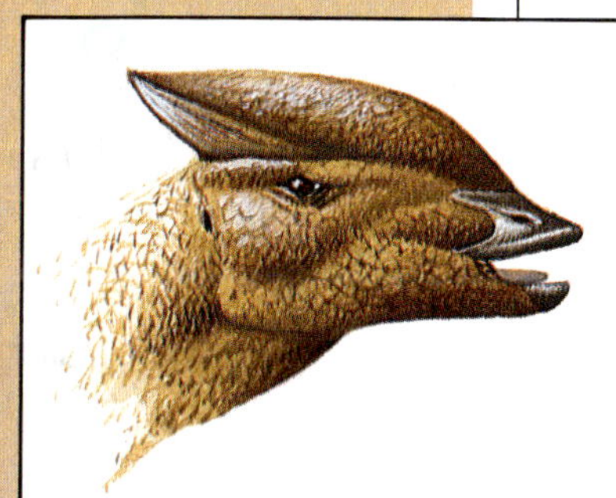

PARASAUROLOPHUS WALKERI

'ALMOST A RIDGED LIZARD'
ORNITHOPODA, HADROSAURID
LATE CRETACEOUS
ALBERTA, CANADA, NEW MEXICO AND UTAH, USA

Parasaurolophus was first described by William Parks in 1923 from remains found in Alberta, Canada.

As with most other duckbills, an adult *Parasaurolophus* reached a length of about 9 metres (30 feet) and probably weighed about 4400 kilograms (5 tons).

The snouts of the hollow-crested duckbills were narrower than those of the flat-headed duckbills or those with solid crests. This probably meant that they could select delicate morsels from the vegetation.

The most spectacular of the hollow-crested duckbills was *Parasaurolophus*. Its nose bones were modified into great sweeping hollow tubes that curved away back behind the skull.

What was the purpose of such a structure?

Palaeontologists are not really sure. It was probably some sort of voice amplification system, like the nose flaps on the heads of the crestless duckbills. With such an instrument the animal would have been able to come out with a sound like a trombone, as a mating call or as a warning to others. On the other hand it may have been a device for circulating the air around the skull and keeping the brain cool in hot weather. The flamboyant crest of *Parasaurolophus* may have had yet another function. It may have acted as a kind of foliage deflector as it pushed its way through thick forest – see how the crest seems to fit into a notch in the backbone to produce a very streamlined shape? It may be that all of these theories are true, and that the crest was a multi-purpose structure.

If the crest of *Parasaurolophus* were a signalling structure, it would seem to have been reinforced by the tail. The tail was flattened and very broad, almost like a billboard. The great areas of skin on its sides were probably brightly coloured and patterned to act as warning or a sign of recognition.

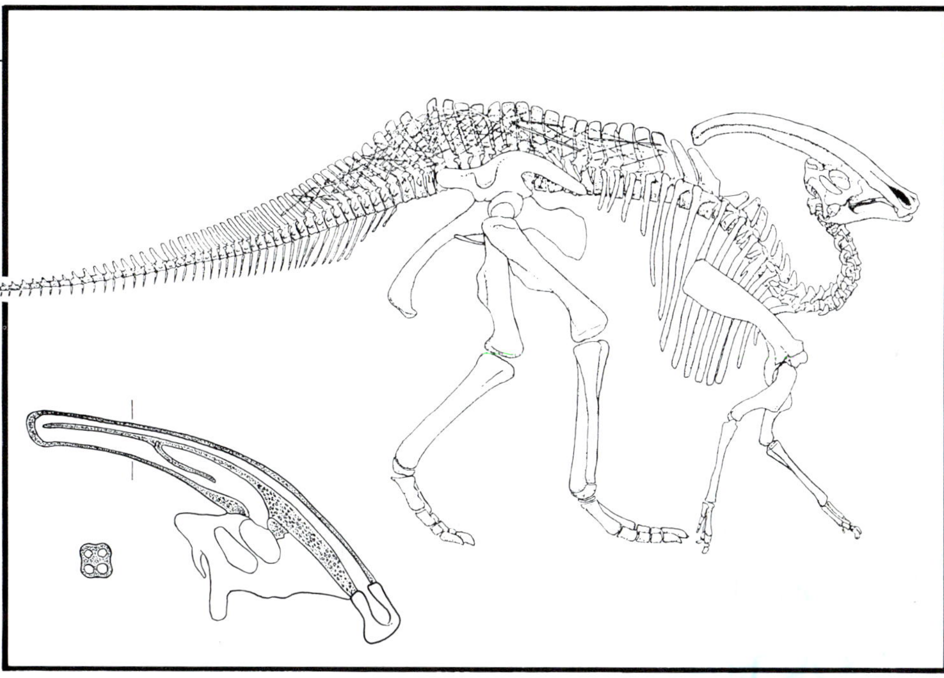

The crest of *Parasaurolophus* was a double tube, sweeping back from the nostrils to the tip, and then forward again into the skull.

The upper Cretaceous forest probably rang with the trumpeting of duckbills during the mating season.

The sleek line of a crested *Parasaurolophus* may have been able to push easily through dense forest.

Remains of a short-crested *Parasaurolophus* have been found. These were probably from a female of the same species.

STEGOCERAS VALIDUS

'VALID HORNED ROOF'
ORNITHOPODA, PACHYCEPHALOSAURID
LATE CRETACEOUS
WESTERN NORTH AMERICA

The first remains to be found were some teeth discovered in 1856. Some skull fragments were found in Alberta, Canada, in 1902 and they were given the name *Stegoceras* by Lawrence Lambe of the Geological Survey of Canada. The most complete skeleton, and indeed the most complete skeleton of any pachycephalosaurid, was found in 1920 in Alberta by Charles Gilmore.

When only the teeth were known, there was some confusion about what the name of the animal should be. The 'valid' part of the name indicates that this is the name that was accepted.

Stegoceras was a medium-sized dinosaur, about 2.5 metres (6 feet 6 inches) in length.

All the pachycephalosaurids were plant-eaters, although some of the teeth were sharp and serrated like carnivore's teeth.

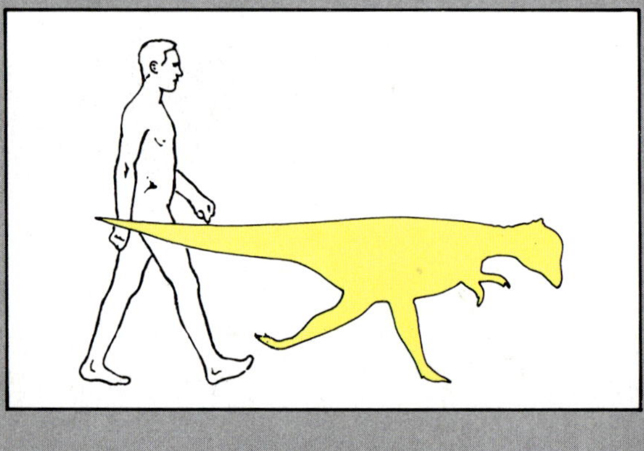

The pachycephalosaurids were the mountain goats of their day. Apart from being about the same size, their serrated teeth show that they ate the same sort of food as goats – tough scrubby mountain plants. They probably lived in herds or flocks, just as goats do, and the males would have competed with one another by banging heads together, the prize being the leadership of the herd.

Usually, dinosaur skulls are quite rare, because they were so lightly built and easily broken. Pachycephalosaurid skulls, on the other hand, are quite common in late Cretaceous rocks, because they were big, solid lumps of bone. Most of their remains are found in river sediments and look as if they had been washed downstream a long way. From this, we deduce that pachycephalosaurids lived up in the mountains.

The solid lump of head bone was used as a battering ram. That is obvious. The rest of the skeleton seems to have been built to back it up, with the back and tail vertebrae strong enough to take the shock of the impact. The female pachycephalosaurs probably did not have such prominent bone growths on the skull.

All the pachycephalosaurids had thickened skulls. *Stegoceras* had the typical dome. *Homalocephale* had a wedge-shaped skull with a thick top, but no prominent dome. *Pachycephalosaurus* is known from some enormous skulls that must have belonged to animals 4.5 metres (15 feet) long.

Although the skeleton of *Stegoceras* is far from complete, enough of it survived to show what the animal looked like.

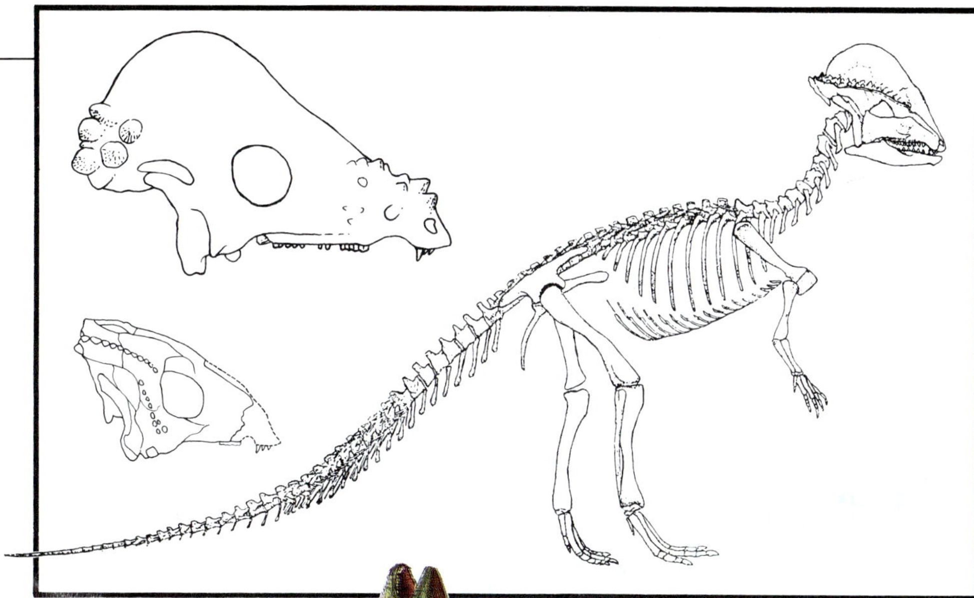

Pachycephalosaurid hips were very wide. This was possibly part of the backbone-strengthening system, or it could show that these dinosaurs bore their young alive, rather than laying eggs.

Stegoceras probably roamed the Cretaceous mountains in herds. The males probably fought each other for leadership of the herd by head-butting.

EUOPLOCEPHALUS TUTUS

'WELL ARMOURED HEAD'

ANKYLOSAURIA, ANKYLOSAURID

LATE CRETACEOUS

ALBERTA, CANADA, AND NORTH-WEST CHINA

The ankylosaurids may have originated in eastern Asia and then spread to North America across the Bering land bridge.

Euoplocephalus remains were first discovered in the Red Deer River area of Alberta, Canada, in 1902 and it was named by Lawrence Lambe in 1910. Since then, more ankylosaur pieces have been found that seem to belong to *Euoplocephalus*. Dr Walter Preston Coombes of Amherst, Massachusetts, has recently re-classified all the ankylosaurs. The most thorough work was done on *Euoplocephalus* in the 1980s by Dr Kenneth Carpenter in Boulder, Colorado, USA, casting away many misconceptions about it and the ankylosaurid group in general.

Euoplocephalus was not the largest of the ankylosaurs, but fully grown it would have reached a length of 5.25 metres (18 feet) and a weight of 2700 kilograms (3 tons).

It was a plant-eater, browsing and grazing close to the ground.

▶ *Euoplocephalus* probably grazed in open country, defending itself with its armour and its club.

'Well armoured head', the Latin name means. And indeed it had one! The bones of the skull were fused into a rigid strongbox-like structure – even the eyelids were armoured, clanging down like shutters when danger threatened. Nor did the armouring stop at the head. As in all the ankylosaurids, the body was covered with armoured knobs and spikes. These were arranged in bands across the back, and the biggest of them formed rows that ran the length of the animal. As a final defensive measure the tail was one gigantic knobkerrie – a long-shafted club with a great heavy weight at the end that could be swung with a shattering blow at an enemy. The beast was the nearest thing to a living tank that has ever evolved.

The head, although looking solid, was actually honeycombed with passages and holes. These were probably used to warm the air as it was breathed in.

The finding of back armour pieces of ankylosaurids is quite common, compared with other dinosaur remains. In a river, a dead ankylosaurid would roll over on its back with the weight of the armour and sink, belly upwards. They are often found in this position.

Other ankylosaurids had different arrangements of armour.

Pieces of armour are usually the only parts of ankylosaur skeletons to be found.

Euoplocephalus had a stout, barrel-like body, covered in armour.

The tail club was made of lumps of bone. The end half of the tail was fused into a rigid shaft that could be swung at an enemy.

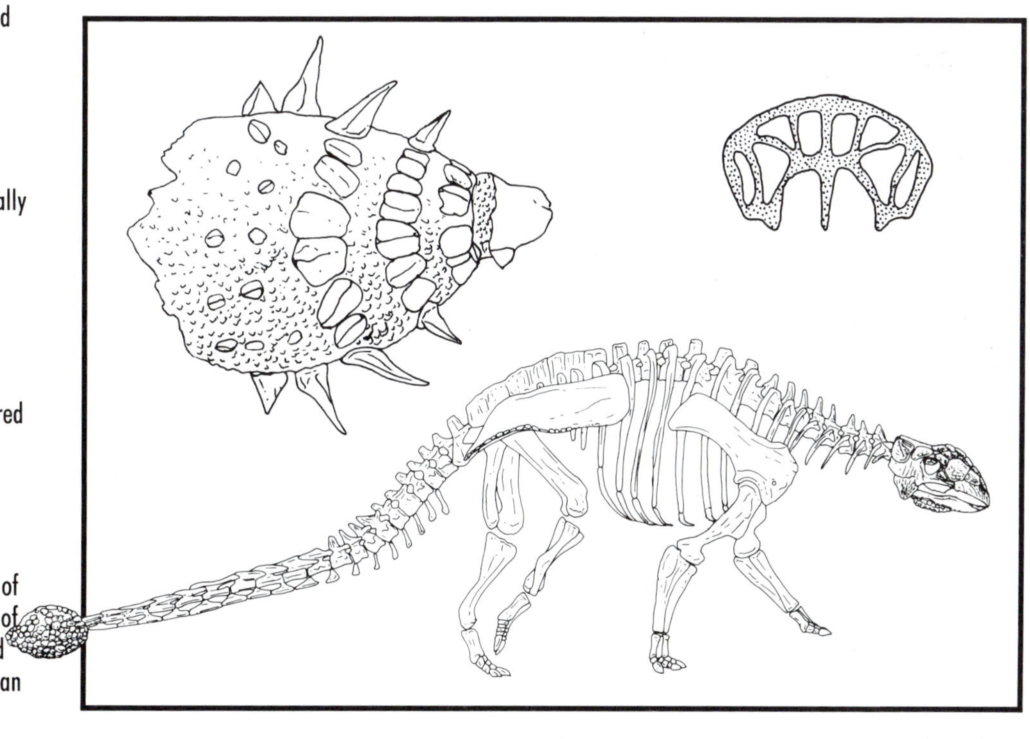

PANOPLOSAURUS MIRUS

'WONDERFUL FULLY ARMOURED LIZARD'
ANKYLOSAURIA, NODOSAURID
LATE CRETACEOUS
NORTH AMERICA

Panoplosaurus was one of the dinosaurs discovered in the Canadian dinosaur rush, which began in 1912. It was described and named by Lawrence Lambe in 1919.

This dinosaur was one of the largest of the nodosaurids, reaching a length of 7 metres (23 feet).

Panoplosaurus was a plant-eater. As a group, the nodosaurids had narrower jaws than their relatives, the ankylosaurids. This probably meant that they were more selective about the kind of food they ate.

The armoured ankylosaurs were divided into two groups – the ankylosaurids, with an armour consisting of plates rather than spikes and a bony club at the end of the tail, and the nodosaurids that seemed to go in for spiky armour and had no tail club. *Panoplosaurus* was a typical nodosaurid. Flat plates covered the back in rows that ran crossways. These were particularly broad in the shoulder and neck region. In this the animal resembled the ankylosaurids, but at the sides there were massive spikes that stuck out sideways and effectively guarded the flanks. The skull was fully armoured so that it looked just like a bony lump, with no apparent boundaries between the skull bones. The only holes were for the eyes and nostrils.

A feature of ankylosaur skulls in general was the presence of a palate. This shelf of bone separated the mouth cavity from the nose cavity and allowed the animal to eat and breathe at the same time. (We, and all other mammals, have palates like this.) This would suggest that ankylosaurs ate a great deal of food. The great size of the body also suggests that a large volume of food could be processed at one time.

▶ As with all ankylosaurs, the skull and the back armour of *Panoplosaurus* are the most frequently preserved parts of the skeleton.

▶ The nodosaurids probably roamed the late Cretaceous uplands. Their remains are found in rocks formed from river and swamp sediments that gathered on lowlands. The armour was so strong, the bodies could be washed all the way downstream without breaking up.

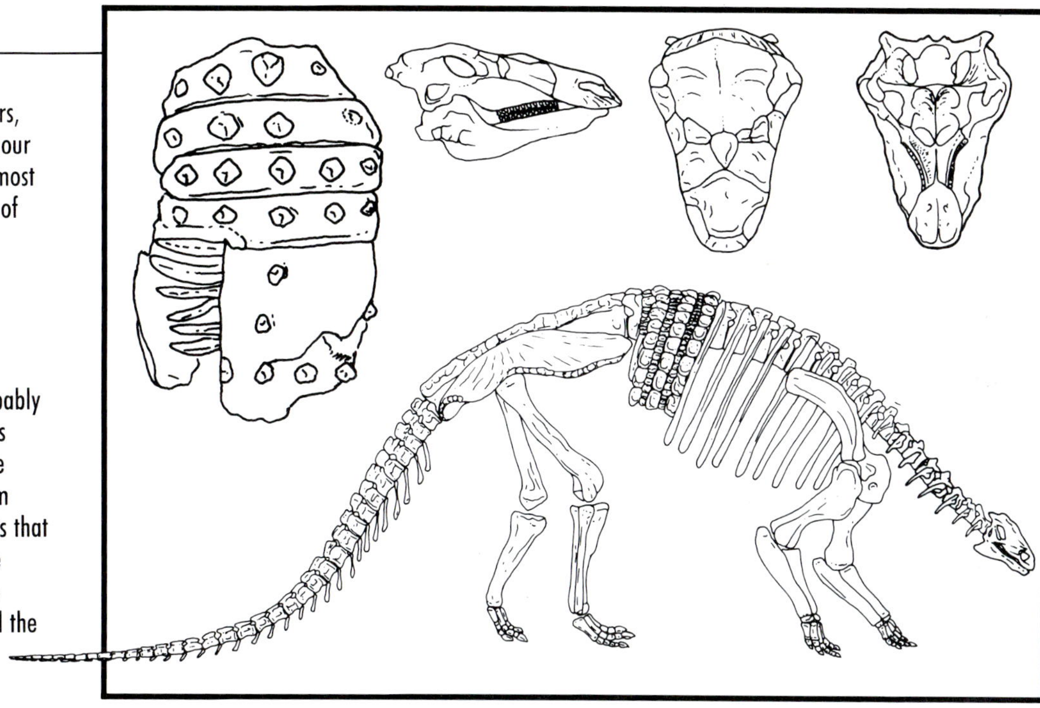

▼ A charging *Panoplosaurus*, all armoured head and spikes, must have been a remarkable sight.

▶ The body probably contained a large volume of intestine to process the food. The tiny teeth could not have chewed very much.

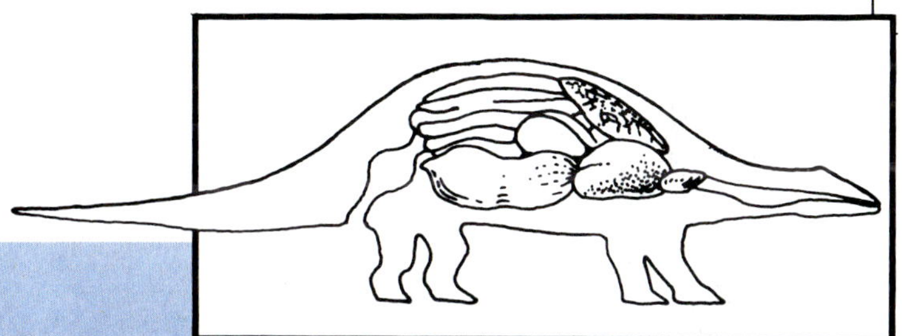

PROTOCERATOPS ANDREWSI

'ANDREWS' EARLY HORNED HEAD'
CERATOPSIA, PROTOCERATOPSID
LATE CRETACEOUS
MONGOLIA

The American Museum of Natural History's expedition to Mongolia in 1922–5 uncovered this skeleton. Over 100 skeletons of *Protoceratops* were found, as well as nests of eggs. The description was published in 1923 by Walter Granger and William K. Gregory.

The species was named after Roy Chapman Andrews, the leader of the expedition.

Protoceratops was small for a ceratopsian, reaching a maximum of 2.7 metres (9 feet).

Its jaw arrangement shows *Protoceratops* to have had a powerful bite. Its teeth were evolved for chopping rather than chewing. Its barrel-shaped body probably contained a big gut. All these suggest that *Protoceratops* ate tough plant material.

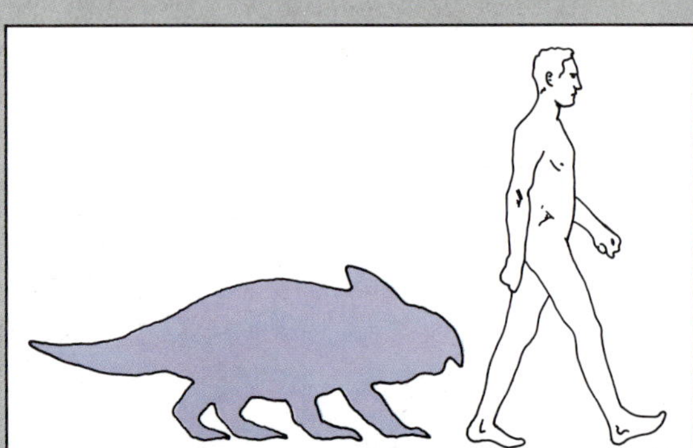

▼ *Protoceratops* did not have the spectacular horns of the later ceratopsians, but old males may have developed a short horny growth above the massive beak.

By the late Cretaceous the ceratopsians began to grow large, heavy at the front end, and, unlike their ancestors, such as *Psittacosaurus*, came down on all fours. *Protoceratops* was one of the first to do this. The neck frill was very big and contained gaping holes. The edges of the holes provided anchor points for the strong jaw muscles – the neck frill had not yet developed into the armour shield of the later ceratopsians.

The most important thing about the Mongolian find – at the romantically named Flaming Cliffs in the Gobi Desert – was the fact that *Protoceratops* nests, full of eggs, were found there as well. The eggs were almost sausage-shaped and arranged in circles pointing outwards. This was the first time that anybody had found proof that the dinosaurs actually laid eggs. As well as that, the site threw up all sorts of other details about *Protoceratops* life. A small egg-stealing ostrich dinosaur, *Oviraptor*, was found in a nest, suffocated by the same sandstorm that had buried and killed the eggs. A sickle-clawed meat-eater, *Velociraptor*, (p. 102–3) was found locked in deadly struggle with an adult *Protoceratops*.

Although it walked on all fours *Protoceratops* forelimbs were shorter than the hind limbs. This suggests that it was not far away from its bipedal ancestors.

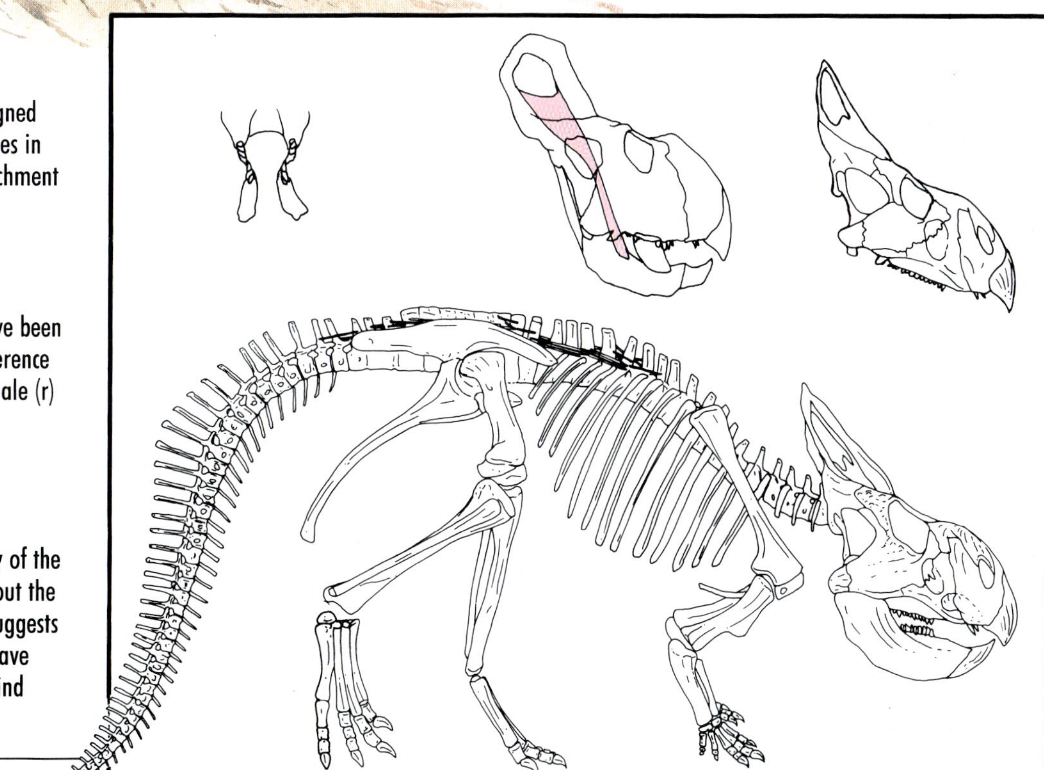

The teeth were designed for chopping, and the holes in the frill were for the attachment of strong jaw muscles.

Enough remains have been found to show us the difference between male (l) and female (r) skulls.

The centre of gravity of the body was far back, at about the region of the hips. This suggests that *Protoceratops* may have been able to take to its hind legs sometimes.

CHASMOSAURUS BELLI

'BELL'S CLEFT LIZARD'
CERATOPSIA, CERATOPSID
LATE CRETACEOUS
ALBERTA, CANADA

The first remains of *Chasmosaurus* to be found, in 1902, were thought to be from a short-frilled ceratopsian, *Monoclonius*. Complete skulls were found in Alberta by Charles Sternberg and his sons in 1913 and described by Lawrence Lambe of the Canadian Geological Survey in 1914. Since then, several skulls have been found. These differ from one another, and so they may represent different species of *Chasmosaurus*, or different sexes and ages of individuals of the same species.

Chasmosaurus was the earliest of the long-frilled ceratopsians.

It reached a length of 5 metres (17 feet) and a weight of 3600 kilograms (4 tons).

Long-frilled ceratopsians had longer faces and jaws than the short-frilled types. Possibly, they could be more selective about the plants they ate.

The long-frilled ceratopsians differed from their short-frilled counterparts by the size of the frill and the arrangement of horns on the head. The frill size was taken to an extreme in *Chasmosaurus*. The neck frill was extended well over the shoulders as a great triangular structure. The holes in it were so large that we could hardly call the structure a shield. Made of struts of bone covered in skin, it would have been more like a sail. As for its function, perhaps 'flag' would be more appropriate than 'sail'. With a big area of head like this to 'wave' at an opponent or an enemy, *Chasmosaurus* must have been a formidable sight.

Although the brow horns of some species of *Chasmosaurus*, for example *C. kaiseni*, were quite long, those of *C. belli* were short and could not have been used very well as defensive weapons. It is quite possible, however, that the long-horned types were actually males and the short-horned types were the females of the same species. We cannot be sure.

▼ *Chasmosaurus* herds may have been defended by the males, all facing outwards and presenting an intimidating area of frill towards an enemy.

The huge heart-shaped frill of *Chasmosaurus* distinguished it from other ceratopsians.

As well as the frill being bigger, the skull was longer and narrower than that of a typical short-frilled ceratopsian.

Other long-frilled ceratopsians, such as *Torosaurus*, had very long frills and long brow horns.

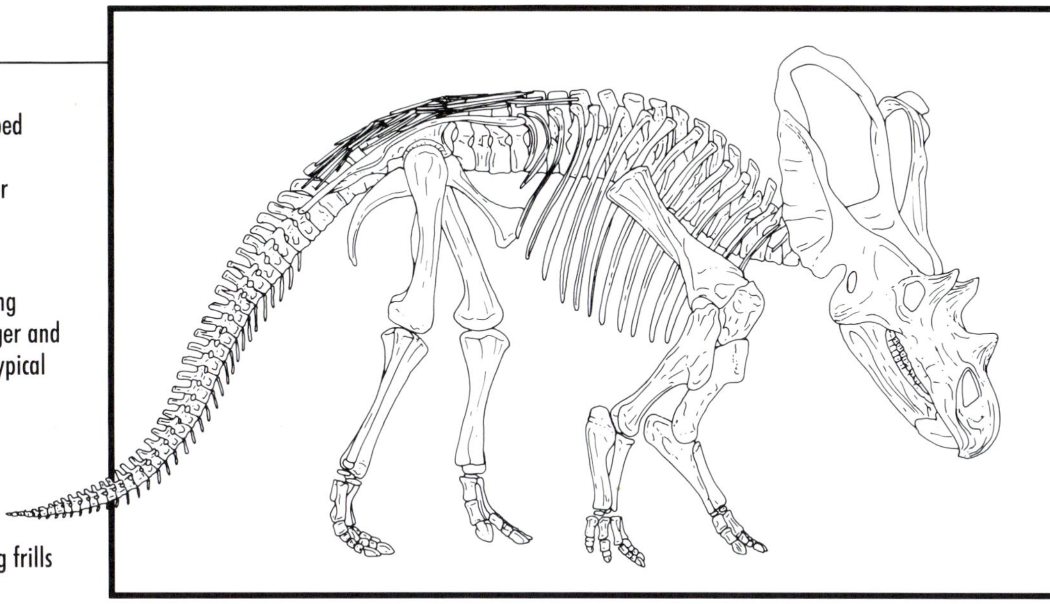

The frill may well have been brightly patterned to draw attention to its size.

STYRACOSAURUS ALBERTENSIS

'SPIKED LIZARD FROM ALBERTA'
CERATOPSIA, CERATOPSID
LATE CRETACEOUS
ALBERTA, CANADA, AND MONTANA, USA

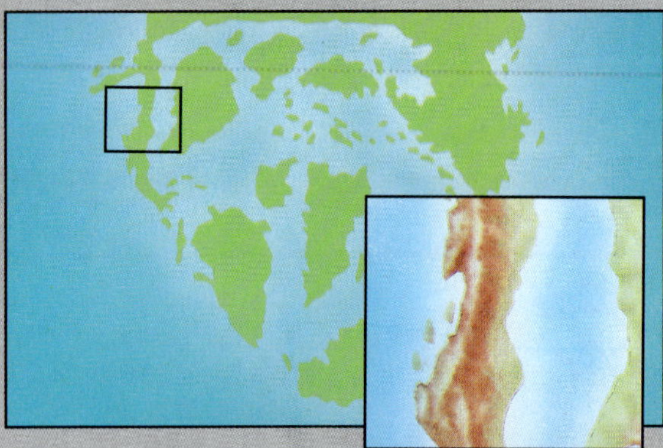

In 1913, an expedition was mounted by the Geological Survey of Canada to try to prevent the well-organized teams from the American Museum of Natural History from unearthing and carting away all the Canadian dinosaur remains. Charles Sternberg and this three sons brought out many late Cretaceous dinosaurs from the Red Deer River area, including the first *Styracosaurus*. The horned dinosaur was then described by Lawrence Lambe of the Geological Survey of Canada that same year.

Styracosaurus reached a length of about 5.5 metres (18 feet) and weighed about 3500 kilograms (4 tons).

The food of *Styracosaurus*, and probably the other advanced ceratopsians, may have consisted primarily of the fern-like cycad leaves.

The ceratopsids were divided into two main lines of evolution. There was the short-frilled evolutionary line, and the long-frilled evolutionary line. *Styracosaurus* belonged to the short-frilled. Most of the short-frilled line had a single long horn on the nose and a short neck frill. Some had short horns above the eyes and some had not. *Styracosaurus* had the single horn, but it differed from the other short-frilled ceratopsians in the shape of the neck frill. The rim of the frill was drawn out into six huge spikes, giving it the appearance of an Indian chief's head-dress.

Like the chief's head-dress its function would have been to terrify and to intimidate. When the animal turned its head towards you, the spikes would stick out around it in a very alarming manner, and if the *Styracosaurus* charged, then the hurtling creature would look even larger and more dangerous than it really was. The spikes were probably also useful in protecting the neck, but when it came to fighting, the long horn would have been the main weapon.

Family groups of short-frilled ceratopsians have been discovered. It looks as if they had some kind of family structure, with the adults looking after the youngsters until they were well grown.

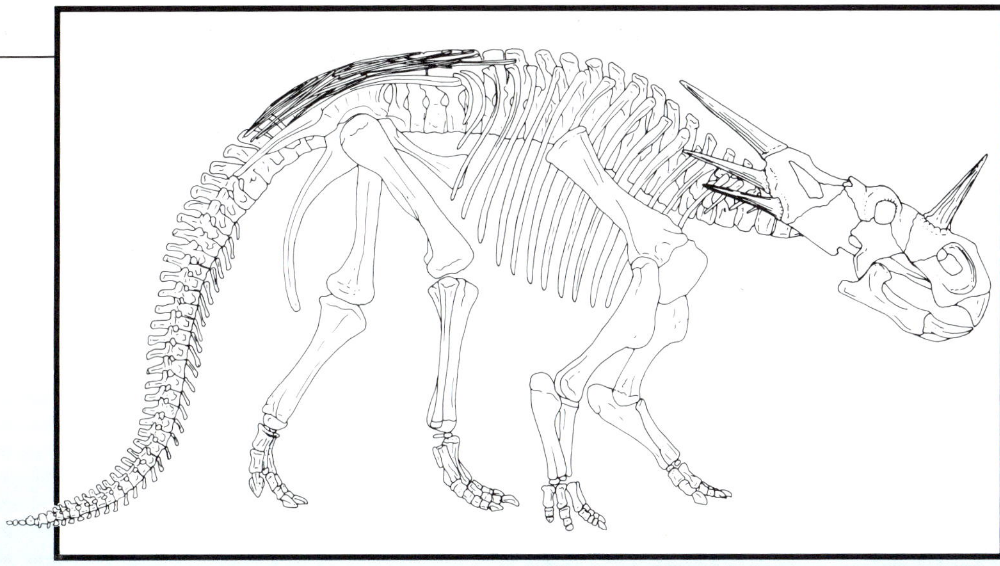

◀ The ceratopsian skeleton was very powerful around the shoulders and forelimbs. It needed to be, to support the great weight of the head.

▼ The spiked neck frill of *Styracosaurus* must have been a terrifying sight.

TRICERATOPS HORRIDUS

'HORRIBLE THREE-HORNED HEAD'
CERATOPSIA, CERATOPSID
LATE CRETACEOUS
COLORADO, NORTH AND SOUTH DAKOTA, USA, SASKATCHEWAN AND ALBERTA, CANADA

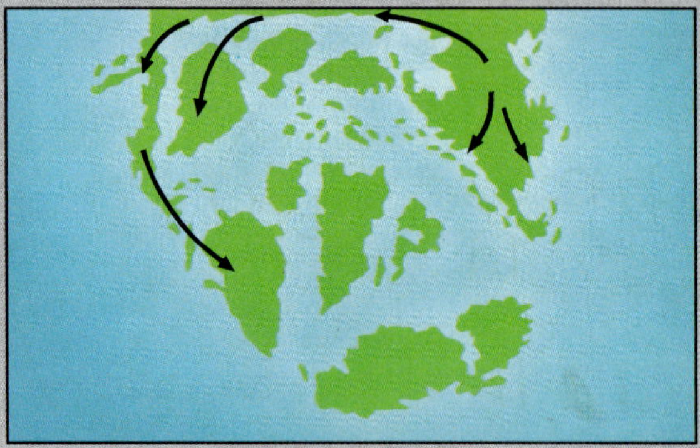

After many unidentifiable fragments had been found in the 1850s, 60s and 70s, the first certain *Triceratops* remains came to light in 1887 with a pair of horn cores (the bone around which horns are formed). Othniel Charles Marsh – usually so right in these things – thought that they came from a buffalo. In 1888, a complete skull was discovered on a ranch in Wyoming, USA, and taken to Marsh by John Bell Hatcher, a professional collector. It was described and published by Marsh in 1889.

Triceratops was the biggest of the ceratopsians, reaching a length of 9 metres (30 feet), 2 metres (7 feet) of which was skull. It may have weighed something like 10 500 kilograms (12 tons).

It was a plant-eater, browsing near the ground.

Triceratops was the biggest of the horned dinosaurs. The bulls may have competed with one another for leadership of the herd by locking horns and shoving, like bison do today.

The best-known of the short-frilled ceratopsians is also the largest. It also breaks some of the group's rules. Whereas most short-frilled types had only a single long nose horn, *Triceratops* had quite a short nose horn and a massive pair of horns over the eyes. Most short-frilled ceratopsians had holes in the neck frill – *Triceratops* had a neck frill that was a solid sheet of armoured bone. It was as if the frill had given up all pretence of being an anchor for the jaw muscles and had become a vast warlike shield instead.

We know a great deal about the head of *Triceratops*. Usually dinosaur skulls are scarce, because they consist of flimsy frameworks of bony struts and are easily broken in the fossilization process. A *Triceratops* skull, on the other hand, was a massive chunk of solid bone and withstood anything that geology could throw at it. As a result, we have identified about 15 different *Triceratops* species, all based on slight differences in the structure of the skull.

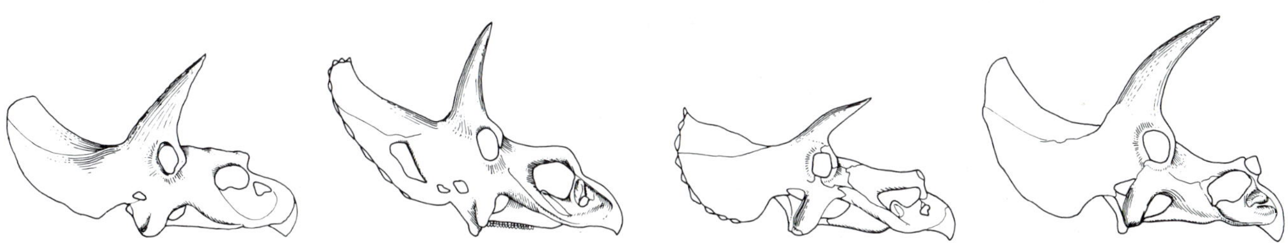

▲ Many different species of *Triceratops* are known, from their different skulls.

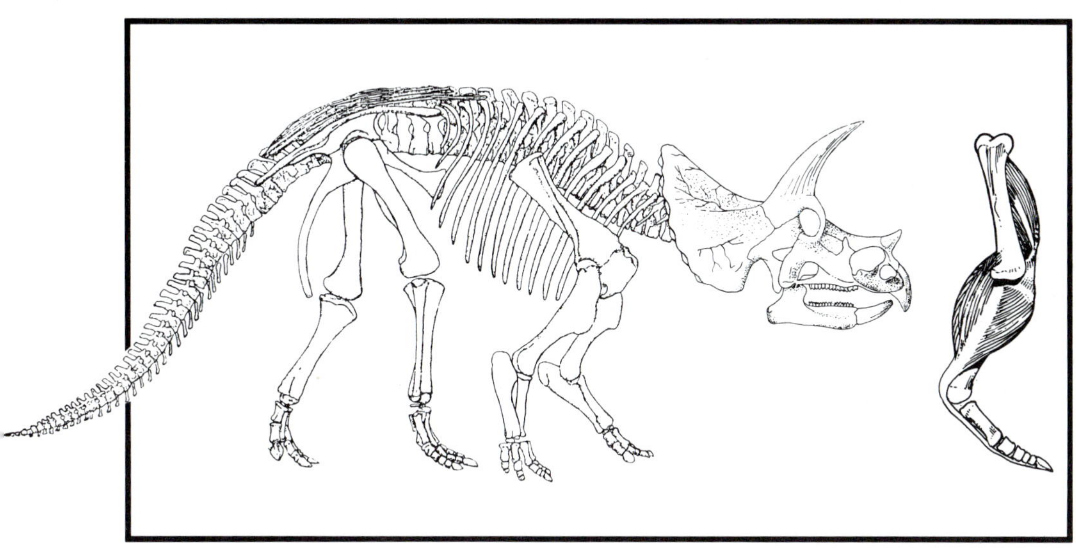

◄ The legs were very powerful to keep the massive weight off the ground. Ridges and sockets on the bones show where the muscles were attached.

EXTINCTION

And then there were none!

At the end of the Cretaceous, 65 million years ago, nature drew a curtain. All dinosaurs, all pterosaurs, all the wondrous sea reptiles, as well as all sorts of other animals on land and in the sea, were wiped from the face of the Earth. The magnificent array of reptilian life that had existed for 150 million years suddenly disappeared. The disappearance was sudden. Rocks of the late Cretaceous are full of the fossils of all different types of these wonderful creatures, and then the rocks that were laid down immediately above them are barren.

Why?

We don't know, but here are a few theories.

Many people believe that the agent of destruction came from space. The first 'extraterrestrial' theory involved the explosion of a star somewhere close to us in the galaxy. This could have bathed the Earth in deadly cosmic radiation, killing off many of the creatures that lived there. Such an explosion could also have produced clouds of cosmic dust which, when passing through the solar system, could have dimmed the sun so that temperatures on the Earth fell. This theory is not widely accepted at the moment.

A more spectacular extraterrestrial theory is that the Earth was hit by some massive object at that time. This could have been a huge meteorite up to about 9 miles (15 km) in diameter. This would have disintegrated in a vast explosion and would have sent up clouds of dust and gas into the atmosphere. The sky would have become dark for months, and plants would have died off. Plant-eating dinosaurs would have starved, and the meat-eaters feeding on them would also have died.

It may not have been a meteorite; it could have been a series of comets. The Earth seems to pass through a thick belt of comets every 26 million years or so, and the timing would be right. The evidence for these theories comes from a bed of rock at the very top of the Cretaceous. This rock is rich in the rare metal iridium, which is uncommon on the surface of the Earth but more often found in meteorites or comets. Iridium dust would have been scattered around after the landing of a meteorite or a comet, and would have collected in the sediments formed at the time. On the other hand, if

▼ It is possible that the dinosaurs were wiped out by a massive explosion that resulted when a huge meteorite collided with the Earth. The smoke and dust produced would have altered the climate so much that all life on the planet would have been affected.

there were a large number of volcanoes active at this time their dust could have produced the iridium layer from material below the Earth's crust.

Many other palaeontologists believe that the extinction was more gradual than this. By 'gradual', we mean something of the order of a million years or so. To us a million years seems an incredible length of time, but in the history of the Earth it would only produce a bed of rock a few centimetres thick. So, anything happening in a million years would look as if it were very sudden in the fossil record.

The late Cretaceous was a time of changing landscapes. The sea levels may have risen, spreading shallow seas across areas of continent that had, up to then, been dry. This would have brought cooler and changeable weather to many areas, and the big animals that were more used to the warm conditions may not have been able to cope with this and died out. This would account for the change in fossil plants that can also be seen in the late Cretaceous rocks. On the other hand, the sea levels may have lowered. Areas that were once shallow sea bottoms became dry land, and animals would have been able to wander from one continent across to another. This would mean that an animal would find its food eaten up by some newcomer from somewhere else. The newcomer would also have brought diseases and parasites with it, diseases and parasites to which it was immune but to which the other animals would have had no resistance. Another result of the lowering of the sea level would have been that, with a smaller area of sea, there was a small number of sea plants that could convert the carbon dioxide of the air into oxygen. The carbon dioxide would then have built up in the atmosphere, producing much warmer climates. The dinosaurs would have been as vulnerable to conditions that were too warm as they would have been to conditions that were too cold. This lower sea level idea would account for the extinctions of sea animals at the time as well. And with less sedimentary matter producing fewer sedimentary rocks in the sea, any iridium present at the time would appear unnaturally concentrated.

All these theories have their supporters and the arguments will go on for as long as there are palaeontologists studying the subject. For now, we can accept that there was some kind of biological crisis that marked the end of the Cretaceous period. This crisis wiped out the dinosaurs, the pterosaurs, the mosasaurs, the plesiosaurs, and many of the sea-living invertebrates such as the ammonites and the belemnites as well. It left untouched other reptiles such as the crocodiles, the turtles, the lizards and the snakes. More importantly, it left untouched the small furry mammals that had lived, scurrying unnoticed about the feet of the great dinosaurs for 150 million years. These were then able to develop and expand, and to take over where the dinosaurs had left off. The age of reptiles was over. The age of mammals had begun.

A clue to the dinosaurs' disappearance may lie in a bed rich in the rare metal iridium that lies at the top of the Cretaceous rocks.

LIFE SINCE THE DINOSAURS

Tertiary

Despite the biological upheavals that had brought the Cretaceous period to a close 65 million years ago, the slow, trundling movements of the continents continued.

At the beginning of the period the climates were everywhere warm and humid. Tropical forests and jungles were the main types of habitat, and some very strange animals indeed lived amongst them. It was the beginning of the Age of Mammals. The great reptiles had newly gone and the mammals flourished and diversified to take their place. Up to then, the mammals had all been small, shrew-like creatures – insignificant and unnoticed. Then they expanded to take over the livelihoods of the extinct reptiles. Whales evolved to live in the sea. Bats evolved to fly, although the birds were already well established in this role. All kinds of habitats on land were occupied by new mammals. It was as if nature were trying out all kinds of different animal shapes to see what would be most successful. Most of the mammals of that time would appear very bizarre to us today, but there were also those that would seem fairly familiar.

About half way through the Tertiary, conditions began to change. The climate became cooler and the dense forests gave way to prairies, steppes, pampas and savannas. This was something quite new. There had been no areas of open grassland before. The animal life evolved accordingly. To eat something as tough and indigestible as grass an animal needs particularly hard-wearing teeth and a complex stomach. To live on the open plains the animal needs long legs, so that it can run away from enemies. So, as the grasslands spread throughout the world in the mid-Tertiary, so there evolved the horses, the antelopes and the camels (the camels first evolved as grassland, not desert, animals) to live on them.

In isolated places like South America and Australia, evolution went its own way. The same variety of animals evolved, but from different stocks. Amongst the strange mammals of South America there evolved a creature that looked very much like a small horse. This was no relation to the horse but it had evolved the same shape and adaptations to live in the same grassland habitat as the horses elsewhere. In Australia the kangaroos evolved for exactly the same reason. Have you ever noticed how similar the head of a kangaroo is to the head of an antelope? The same way of life – in this case eating grass and moving quickly across the plains – produces the same shapes over and over again. This concept is known as 'convergent evolution'.

Towards the end of the period the climates started to become rather cooler, as a build-up to the Ice Age.

▶ The early Tertiary was a time of tropical forests. Mammals expanded rapidly to take over from the dinosaurs that had recently died out, and all kinds of mammal shapes evolved. There were plant-eating mammals, flesh-eating mammals, and even flying and swimming mammals. Some of their shapes would be familiar to us today, but others would be extremely strange.

▲ Grasslands spread over the world in the late Tertiary, replacing the forests. The grasses and the open landscapes they produced gave rise to new kinds of mammals – long-legged running types with complex stomachs that could digest these tough plants.

Quaternary

The last fragment of geological time – the Quaternary – is very short. It is, however, quite important to us, since it covers the arrival of perhaps the most influential life-form that has evolved on our planet so far – Man.

The Quaternary started a mere 1.7 million years ago – the day before yesterday in geological terms. It can be divided into the Ice Age (or the Pleistocene) and the Recent – note the capital R. The Recent is that period from about 20 000 years ago to the present day.

During the short period of time of the Quaternary there has not been much opportunity for continental movement. However, the changes in climate have been tremendous. The cooling that took place in the later part of the Tertiary reached a climax in the Ice Age when glaciers and ice sheets spread southwards from the North Pole, covering Canada, northern Europe and much of northern Asia.

The ice did not cover the whole world. Nor did the ice cover the affected areas all the time. It came and went, several times.

Animal life evolved to cope with these conditions. For the glacial conditions many animals grew large – a large animal keeps its heat in better than a small one – and developed shaggy coats as insulation. Mammoth and woolly rhinoceros roamed the cold tundra regions surrounding the edges of the ice sheets. In more southerly regions there were large mammals as well. The South American grasslands had giant ground sloths that stood 6 metres (20 ft) high, and glyptodonts – like armadilloes as big as motor cars.

Specialized meat-eaters evolved to feed on the very large animals. The sabre-toothed cats of North America and Europe developed their long stabbing fangs to cut through the thick skin of the elephantine animals that were around at the time.

With the final retreat of the ice, human beings spread over the world. They hunted the animals, sometimes to extinction, cleared woodlands and forests for settlement and agriculture, and tamed the herds of grass-eaters.

▼ We are sometimes lucky enough to find the entire bodies of recently extinct animals as fossils. Mammoths often sank into Pleistocene bogs. Their bodies were frozen in the mud and preserved.

THE FIRST DISCOVERIES

EARLIEST DINOSAUR DISCOVERIES

It can't be easy, picking up a scrap of fossilized bone and trying to reconstruct the whole extinct animal from it. It must have been so much more difficult two hundred years ago, when nobody had any idea of what a dinosaur was. At first, the large bones were taken to be those of human beings – sometimes giant human beings – that existed before the Deluge, or Noah's Flood. In 1731, the well-preserved skeleton of a fossil giant salamander was identified as that of a sinner drowned in the Deluge! Elephant bones found near Paris, France, were generally accepted to have been those of giants. Even today, with the knowledge that we now have, the same mistake is made from time to time. One of the foremost dinosaur experts of this century thought that he had found the tooth of a fossil man – it was the tooth of a pig!

The first fossil of a giant reptile to have been identified as such was a set of jawbones full of wicked teeth, discovered in a quarry in the Netherlands in 1770. They were identified by an anatomist as those of a giant lizard. Then, in 1795, the anatomist George Cuvier proclaimed that it was some kind of a huge sea lizard. Several years later the Reverend William Conybeare, a British expert in fossil sea reptiles, named the creature *Mosasaurus*, or 'reptile from the Meuse', after the area in which it was found.

Dr Gideon Mantell and his wife, Mary, found the first remains of *Iguanodon* in Sussex in about 1818. These were the first remains of a plant-eating dinosaur to be studied scientifically.

Dean William Buckland published the first description of a dinosaur, the jawbone of *Megalosaurus*, in 1824, although the fossil was actually named by his colleague James Parkinson.

THE 1880s

The dinosaur bones found in Britain in the first half of the 19th century were only odd fragments. With nothing to compare them with, it was impossible to make an accurate reconstruction of the full skeleton.

Then, in 1858, a number of fossils, including an almost entire skeleton, were discovered in New Jersey, USA. They were studied closely by Joseph Leidy, a professor of anatomy, and he noticed that the front limbs were much shorter than the back. From this he deduced that the animal must have stood on its hind legs, rather like a kangaroo or a bird. The remains turned out to be those of one of the duck-billed dinosaurs – *Hadrosaurus*, which was very similar to *Anatosaurus* (p 108–9). It was the first time that anyone had an inkling that dinosaurs were not necessarily four-footed animals and from that time it was possible to restore *Iguanodon* and *Megalosaurus* as two-footed creatures.

Then, as if to confirm it, in 1878 there was a remarkable find in a coal mine in Bernissart in Belgium, when a veritable graveyard of *Iguanodon*, with at least 39 skeletons, most of them complete, was found. The *Iguanodon* skeletons from this mine were extracted and reconstructed as two-footed animals – like birds.

In the second half of the 19th century the most remarkable dinosaur discoveries were made in North America by the expeditions of two men – Othniel Charles Marsh and Edward Drinker Cope. Marsh was a professor at Yale, while Cope was an independent scientist of private means. There was no cooperation between these two men. In fact, they loathed one another. Each sent expeditions out West, into pioneer country, following up reports of fossil bones being found in the foothills of the Rockies. Each one made offers of money to anyone

A remarkable find of several dozen complete *Iguanodon* skeletons was made in a Belgian coal mine in 1878. The bodies had been washed into a hollow and preserved in a mass.

Huge dinosaur discoveries were made in the foothills of the Rockies in the 1880s. Much of the excavation was carried out by the rival expeditions of two scientists, Othniel Charles Marsh (top) and Edward Drinker Cope (bottom).

finding significant fossils, to try to ensure that the remains were kept out of the rival's hands, and several times the opposing expeditions came to blows. They even smashed up fossils that had to be left in the field, in case they fell into the other's possession. Most of the finds were made in the Morrison Formation at the foot of the Rocky Mountains. These are late Jurassic in age and represent the river and lake deposits on a fertile floodplain that supported a wide range of dinosaur life.

The standard methods of dinosaur bone extraction, still used today, were pioneered on these expeditions. Each bone, as soon as it was removed, was encased in a protective sleeve of plaster before being transported back to the laboratory for detailed study. As a result of all this frantic activity and fighting, 136 new species of dinosaur were discovered before the century was out. Even now, palaeontologists are still trying to sort out some of the vast volume of dinosaur bones that were brought back at this time.

In 1811, eleven-year-old Mary Anning and her brother Joseph were collecting shells and fossils for their widowed mother to sell in her tourist store in Lyme Regis, in southern England, when they found the skull of a 5-metre (17-foot) fossil sea reptile called *Ichthyosaurus*.

The study of dinosaurs really started in England in the early 1800s. A jawbone with teeth was discovered near Oxford by William Buckland, and named *Megalosaurus*, or 'big reptile', by his friend James Parkinson. A description of this fossil was published in 1824. In about 1818 a country doctor, Gideon Mantell, and his wife, Mary, started to collect fossil bones and teeth from a quarry in Sussex. The most significant of these were some leaf-shaped teeth that were eventually identified as being like the teeth of a modern iguana lizard. The name *Iguanodon*, or 'iguana tooth', was given to this animal in 1825.

It was not until 1841 that the name 'dinosaur' was first invented. This was done by the brilliant anatomist and palaeontologist, Richard Owen. He saw that such creatures as *Megalosaurus* (p 78–9) and *Iguanodon* (p 86–7), and a more recently discovered creature, *Hylaeosaurus*, were so much different from modern reptiles that he put them in a new sub-order of classification, the Dinosauria. This classification is no longer valid but the term 'dinosaur' is still used – in fact it is indispensable – today as the popular term covering these animals.

MODERN DISCOVERIES

By the early years of this century, Canada was the place to look for dinosaurs. Barnum Brown, a fossil collector working for the American Museum of Natural History and who had just uncovered several skeletons of *Tyrannosaurus* (p. 98–9) in Montana, began to explore the Red Deer River in Alberta. There he found skeletons of duck-billed dinosaurs. The Canadian authorities, not to be outdone, then hired Charles Sternberg to hunt for fossils on their behalf. Sternberg had previously worked for Cope, and on this expedition he was joined by his sons. They found a great many duck-billed dinosaurs, carnivorous dinosaurs and armoured dinosaurs, including *Styracosaurus* (p. 124–5).

◀ An excavation team from Germany worked at the dinosaur site at Tendaguru in German East Africa (now Tanzania) between 1909 and 1912. One of the skeletons recovered, the *Brachiosaurus* skeleton in the Humboldt Museum, East Berlin, is the biggest mounted dinosaur skeleton in existence.

In 1909 an expedition from Berlin Museum, led by Werner Janensch, went to a remote place called Tendaguru in German East Africa (now Tanzania) to follow up stories of fossil bones found by miners there. The result was the excavation of a vast sequence of rocks, very much like the American Morrison Formation, and containing a similar collection of animals. These included *Brachiosaurus* (p. 64–5) and *Kentrosaurus* (p. 72–3).

In the 1920s the hunt was on for fossil Man. One expedition to try to find Man's origins was the Central Asiatic Expedition from the American Museum of Natural History, led by Roy Chapman Andrews. They did not find early man, but instead came up with an impressive collection of dinosaurs from the dry wastes of the Gobi desert. These included *Protoceratops*(p. 120–1) and their nests – the first time dinosaur eggs had been found – and *Velociraptor* (p. 102–3).

By now, all the continents were being scoured for dinosaur remains. China began the dinosaur search quite late, but between the 1940s and 1970s Chinese excavations had produced so many dinosaur skeletons that about a quarter of all the dinosaurs we know are of Chinese origin. These include *Mamenchisaurus* (p. 68–9) and many others. They are so much like the North American dinosaurs, we can say that the same conditions existed over the whole of the northern hemisphere during Mesozoic times.

Today, the hunt for fossil animals goes on. However, the big international expeditions are becoming more and more difficult to organize. A big expedition is very difficult to mount, and money is in short supply. There are political problems, too. Many of the potentially good dinosaur sites are in remote corners of developing countries – countries whose governments tend to be suspicious of international teams

▲ The Central Asiatic Expedition, mounted by the American Museum of Natural History, uncovered the first dinosaur eggs, those of *Protoceratops* in the Gobi desert, Mongolia, in 1922.

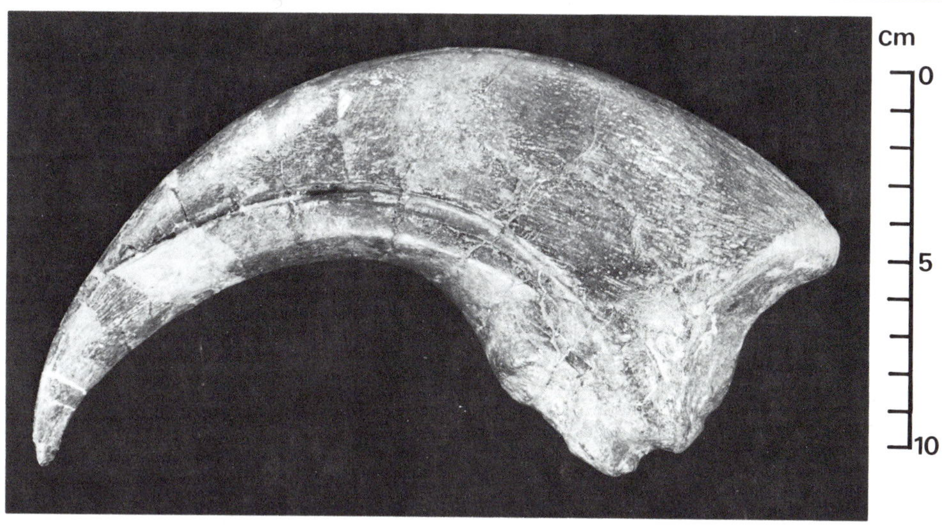

▶ The most exciting find in recent years was that of *Baryonyx* in 1983. The first bone was found by an amateur fossil collector. The animal belonged to a new family of dinosaur.

poking about along their borders. The members of the International Palaeontological Expedition spent Christmas 1977 behind bars in a Nigerian jail because of a misunderstanding about their purpose.

However, the day of the startling discovery made by an amateur did not pass away with Mary Anning and the Mantells. As recently as 1983 an amateur fossil hunter, William Walker, found some bones in a clay-pit in Surrey, England. A team from the British Museum (Natural History) then excavated the entire skeleton and the result was a completely new type of dinosaur, *Baryonyx* (p. 80–1). Quarrymen and civil engineers often turn up dinosaur remains by accident. The first sauropod footprints in Britain were found by a quarryman in a limestone quarry in Dorset in 1987.

Unfortunately, finds made in quarries or road excavations are often not followed up because of financial or business considerations. One of the most tragic examples of this is the case of the fossil ape *Oreopithecus*. The owners of the brown coal mine in Italy, where the remains were found, would not halt the production of coal to enable excavations to be carried out. As a result, we lost the chance to study an important phase in our own evolution.

STUDYING THE DINOSAUR

When Charles Dickens wrote in the opening chapter of *Bleak House* –

> As much mud in the street, as if the waters had but newly retired from the face of the earth, and it would not be wonderful to meet a Megalosaurus, forty feet long or so, waddling like an elephantine lizard up Holborn Hill.

– he was not visualizing the animal shown on p. 78–9. In 1853, the dinosaur was a fairly new concept and the exact nature of something like *Megalosaurus* was a bit of a mystery. The creature that Dickens imagined would, indeed, have been something like a giant lizard.

Megalosaurus's stablemate, *Iguanodon*, has a history that demonstrates this quite nicely. The Mantells had trouble identifying the teeth and bits of bone that they found in the 1920s. Cuvier himself thought the teeth must have belonged to some kind of rhinoceros. Only when Mantell noticed the similarity between the teeth and those of the iguana did Cuvier realize that they must have belonged to a very large herbivorous reptile. Mantell went away and did his own reconstruction based on the few remains at his disposal. The result looked very much like a 20-metre-long lizard. He placed a bony spike found among the remains on the animal's nose, possibly influenced by Cuvier's original rhinoceros idea. The result

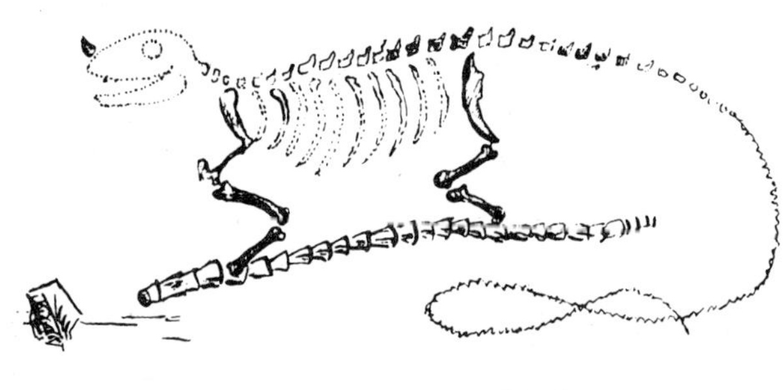

▲ Dr Gideon Mantell produced the first reconstruction of a dinosaur, *Iguanodon*, in the 1820s. Its inaccuracy is understandable when we notice the few bones (shaded) that he actually had to go on.

may look rather odd to us today, but it was the best that could have been done at the time with the information and material available.

The first major dinosaur artist must surely be the British landscape painter John Martin. He is famous for his romantic scenes of biblical catastrophe with mountains toppling upon cities in thunderstorms, and plunging ocean waves sweeping away teeming millions of sinners. In the 1840s he painted a scene of writhing sea serpents for an early book about ichthyosaurs and plesiosaurs by Thomas Hawkins. He also painted *The Country of the Iguanodon*, based on Mantell's studies. In this work, huge dragons fight and tear at one another against a landscape reminiscent of the Tyne Valley in northern England where he had spent

◀ *Iguanodon* and *Megalosaurus* (as visualized by John Martin, the first major dinosaur artist) fighting to the death.

Life-sized statues of *Iguanadon* stand today in Crystal Palace park in London. They were sculpted by animal sculptor Benjamin Waterhouse Hawkins in 1853, and show *Iguanodon* as it was thought to have looked at the time.

The most recent reconstruction of *Iguanodon*, by Dr David Norman of Oxford University, has the creature standing on all fours.

his boyhood. The dragons were, of course, *Iguanodon* and *Megalosaurus* as they were visualized at that time.

After the Great Exhibition in 1851 the Crystal Palace, the huge pavilion of glass and steel built as a centrepiece for it, was moved from Hyde Park to its permanent grounds on a hill in Sydenham, south London. The surrounding parkland was landscaped and, with the enthusiastic approval of Prince Albert, a section of it was set aside to show examples of ancient animals. The animal sculptor Waterhouse Hawkins sculpted the dinosaurs. The results were, predictably, rhinoceros-shaped dragons.

Then, in 1878 the *Iguanodons* were found in the Bernissart mine in Belgium. For the first time, whole *Iguanodon* skeletons were available for study. The horn did not go on the nose, but on the thumb. The length was not as great as at first imagined. The short front legs suggested that the animal went about on two feet. A whole new *Iguanodon* shape appeared – a kind of reptilian giraffe, as King Leopold of Belgium observed at the time. This was the shape of *Iguanodon* that was to be accepted by the public for the next hundred years.

Eventually, in the 1980s, the old image came to be revised again. David Norman at the University Museum, Oxford, England, undertook a whole new study of the animal. He showed that the stiffness of the tail suggested that *Iguanodon* was unlikely to have sat bolt upright using the tail as a prop. What was more, the hands, usually shown as closed fists held in front of the chest, were seen to have been able to spread and take weight, like the toes of a foot. Back went *Iguanodon* on to all fours. The cheek-pouches shown on the restorations of *Iguanodon* and other bird-hipped dinosaurs in this book are, likewise, a recent discovery. So, that is how *Iguanodon* is now portrayed, and will be until the next research shows us something different . . .

It used to be the custom to show the big sauropod dinosaurs, like *Diplodocus* (p. 66–7) and *Brachiosaurus* (p. 64–5), up to their necks in water. The argument was that they needed to be buoyed up to take the weight off their feet, and that the water would give them some protection against meat-eaters. Wrong. New studies of the shape of the bodies show that they were built for a dry land existence – indeed, submerged they would not have been able to breathe against the pressure of the surrounding water. Furthermore, theropod footprints have been found in river sands which show that the big meat-eaters such as *Ceratosaurus* (p. 58–9) could have taken to the water and attacked animals there after all.

The science of palaeontology is in a constant state of evolution. All that a book such as this can do is present the most up-to-date ideas on the subject – ideas that may well be out of date in a decade from now . . .

GLOSSARY

ALGA A water plant with no true stems or leaves. Seaweed is an alga. Plural algae.

AMMONITES The coiled shellfish, now extinct, that were common in Mesozoic seas.

AMPHIBIAN Animal like a frog, able to live on land but laying eggs in water.

ANKYLOSAURS Heavily armoured plant-eating ornithischian dinosaurs of the Jurassic and Cretaceous, e.g. *Euoplocephalus*.

AQUATIC Growing or living in or near water.

ARCHOSAURS Group of reptiles including crocodiles, pterosaurs, ornithischian and saurischian dinosaurs.

BACTERIA A group of microscopic, single-celled organisms.

BIPED Animal that stands and walks on two legs.

BIVALVE Shellfish with a hinged double shell, e.g. cockles, mussels.

BRACHIOPODS Shelled sea creatures mostly extinct, looking like oysters and clams but in no way related.

BROWSERS Animals that feed high up on trees and shrubs.

CALCITE A chalk-like mineral found in the Earth's crust.

CARNIVORE Meat-eating animal.

CARNOSAURS Big meat-eating bipedal saurischian dinosaurs, usually with a short neck and arms, strong legs and huge head, e.g. *Allosaurus*.

CERATOPSIANS Horned ornithischian dinosaurs of the late Cretaceous, e.g. *Triceratops*.

COELUROSAURIDS Meat-eating bipedal saurischian dinosaurs of the late Triassic, usually lightly built, with long neck and small head, e.g. *Coelophysis*.

CONIFERS Cone-bearing trees such as yew, pines and firs.

CONTINENTAL DRIFT The process whereby the Earth's surface is constantly changing due to the constant movement of the independent plates that support the Earth's land masses.

CONVERGENT EVOLUTION The process in which unrelated organisms in the same environment evolve similar structures to perform similar functions.

CRETACEOUS PERIOD The 3rd period of the Mesozoic Era. It lasted from 135 million years ago until about 64 million years ago, when dinosaurs died out.

CYCAD Palm-tree-like plant.

DINOSAURS The popular name for the group of reptiles that comprises saurischians and ornithiscians.

EVOLUTION The process in which the characteristics of groups of organisms change over a series of generations, developing into a different form, in order to adapt to new conditions.

FAUNA The animals that live in a particular area.

FERN A kind of flowerless plant with feathery green leaves.

FLORA The plants that live in a particular area.

FOLIAGE Leaves of a tree or plant.

FORELIMB Front limb (which may be an arm, a leg, a flipper or wing).

FOSSIL The remains or traces of an animal or plant once buried in earth and now hardened like rock.

GINKGO A tree with fan shaped leaves and yellow flowers, found in East Asia.

GRAPTOLITE Sea animal from the Palaeozoic Era consisting of a row of tiny coral-like organisms branching from a stalk.

HADROSAURS Ornithischian dinosaurs of the Late Cretaceous, with a broad bill and often with a crest on the head, e.g. *Parasaurolophus*. Often called the duckbills.

HATCHLING An animal newly hatched from its egg.

HERBIVORE Plant-eating animal.

HORSETAIL Primitive plant, related to the ferns, with whirls of leaves sprouting from a stem at regular intervals.

ICHTHYOSAURS Aquatic reptiles of the Mesozoic Era, with streamlined, fish-shaped bodies.

IGNEOUS ROCK Rock formed by melted matter (e.g. volcanic lava) which has been solidified.

ILIUM The bone forming the upper part of the pelvis and fixed to the backbone.

INVERTEBRATES Animals without a backbone, e.g. insects and shellfish.

ISCHIUM The curved bone forming the base of each half of the pelvis.

JURASSIC PERIOD The 2nd period of the Mesozoic Era. It lasted from 200–135 million years ago.

MAMMAL An animal that can maintain its blood at a constant temperature (i.e. warm-blooded). It gives birth to live young, rather than lays eggs, and suckles them with milk.

MAMMOTH Large extinct elephant with hairy coat and curved tusks.

MESOZOIC ERA The period lasting 225–65 million years ago, which included the Triassic, Jurassic and Cretaceous Periods.

METAMORPHIC ROCK A rock formed when an already existing rock is affected by great heat or pressure and its minerals change.

MINERAL A chemical substance which occurs naturally in the earth.

NOTHOSAURS Aquatic reptiles of the Triassic Period, with lizard-like features.

ORGANISM A living being, an individual animal or plant made up of cells formed into organs or structures.

ORNITHOPODS Ornithischian dinosaurs, with feet like birds' (e.g. *Iguanodon*).

ORNITHISCHIANS The group of dinosaurs characterized by a bird-like hip bone. Includes ornithopods, stegosaurs, ceratopsians, ankylosaurs.

PALAEONTOLOGIST One who studies fossils.

PALAEOZOIC ERA The era before the Mesozoic, lasting from 590–225 million years ago. It included the Cambrian, Ordovician, Silurian, Devonian, Carboniferous and Permian Periods.

PELVIS The hip bones of a skeleton, resting on the legs and supporting the spine.

PELYCOSAURS Primitive reptiles, usually with sails on their backs, living in late Carboniferous and Early Permian times.

PENINSULA A piece of land that is almost surrounded by water.

PLATEAU An area of level high ground.

PLATE TECTONICS The study of the large plates which make up the Earth's crust, and their movements.

PLESIOSAURS Long-necked aquatic reptiles of the Mesozoic Era which swam using large paddle-like legs.

PRECAMBRIAN PERIOD The period up to 590 million years ago, during which the first simple forms of life developed.

PTEROSAURS Flying reptiles of the Mesozoic Era.

PUBIS BONE The bone at the front of the pelvis, usually pointing downward and forward in a reptile.

QUADRUPED An animal that stands and walks on four legs.

REPTILE A scaly-skinned animal whose blood temperature varies according to its surroundings (i.e. cold-blooded). It usually has very short legs (or none at all) and lays eggs.

RESIN A sticky substance that oozes from plants.

RIFT VALLEY A steep-sided valley formed by the sinking of a section of the Earth's crust.

SAURISCHIANS A group of dinosaurs characterized by lizard-like hip bones. Includes the carnosaurs, coelurosaurs and sauropods.

SAUROPODS Huge, plant-eating saurischian dinosaurs with heavy bodies and long necks, e.g. *Apotasaurus*.

SEDIMENTARY ROCK Rock formed from fine particles carried in wind or water and accumulated as sediments.

SPECIES A group of similar animals or plants which can breed together.

STROMATOLITE A series of rocks that were formed by algae, especially in the Precambrian Period.

TENDON A strong band of cord or tissue connecting a muscle to some other part.

TERTIARY PERIOD The time immediately after the Cretaceous Period, in which the mammals developed. It lasted from 65–1.8 million years ago.

THEOCODONTS Early archosaurs of the Permian and Triassic Periods. The immediate ancestors of the dinosaurs.

THEROPODS The group of saurischian dinosaurs which included the coelosaurs and the carnosaurs.

TRIASSIC PERIOD The 1st period of the Mesozoic Era. It lasted from 225–200 million years ago. The dinosaurs appeared towards the end of this period.

VERTEBRAE The individual bones that form the segments of the backbone.

INDEX

E

F

G

H

I

J

K

L

INDEX